Contents

Acknowledgements

I would like to thank Professors Mildred Blaxter, David Donnison, Peter Townsend and Mike Wadsworth for advice, encouragement and criticism during my work on this report.

This kind of work would be impossible without the co-operation and generosity of librarians. In particular, I would like to thank David Potter at Barnardo's and Pat Greenwood at Sussex University. But I am also indebted – as always – to other staff working in the Documents, Information Services and Inter-library loan sections of Sussex University's Library and the University Computing Service.

Several people at Barnardo's including Tessa Baring, Jon Doble, Owen Gill and Mike Hughes were kind enough to read through and make helpful comments on earlier drafts. Lastly, I am particularly grateful to Helen Roberts and Sarah Wellard who have steered this project through to completion and to Nicola Bennett-Jones for her careful editing.

UNFAIR SHARES

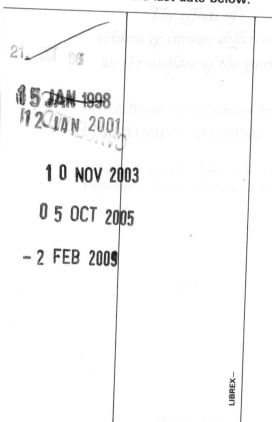

First published in 1994
Reprinted in 1995

© Barnardo's

ISBN: 0 902046 16 0

Published by Barnardo's Publications

Foreword

Barnardo's supports families living in poverty, by providing a range of child welfare services, and by promoting self-help activity. We work in inner city and outlying estates where investment in local communities has practically disappeared. On one estate in Cardiff, Barnardo's helped local people who had no access to affordable credit form a credit union, enabling them to save for vital but expensive purchases like pushchairs, refrigerators and beds. On the same estate, we helped a group of young single mothers set up a cut-price baby goods shop, where they learnt useful skills and developed their self-confidence at the same time as providing a unique service to local parents.

The services provided by organisations like Barnardo's, whilst making a real difference to thousands of children, can only scratch at the surface of the problems which poverty brings with it. We therefore also seek to speak out and promote debate on the key social policy issues affecting children and young people.

While most of us have enjoyed significant increases in income over the past decade, the poorest 10% have suffered a decrease in their income in real terms. (If you count income after housing costs, the bottom 20% have got poorer.) At the same time, there is a widely held perception that society is in crisis. Crime, including juvenile crime is increasing, as is the number of young people convicted for drug offences. The number of young children on child protection registers following serious injuries has risen over the past decade, as has the incidence of teenage suicide. Reading standards amongst seven to eight year olds have declined, and school expulsions increased.

Are these trends connected? Do they reflect a real deterioration in the quality of childrens lives? In this report, Richard Wilkinson argues that there is a causal link between increasing economic inequality and a range of negative phenomena affecting children and young people.

Barnardo's is publishing this report as part of our contribution to this vital debate. It contains some challenging and controversial ideas, which do not necessarily represent the policy position of Barnardo's. However, we believe these ideas merit urgent consideration by policy-makers and everyone concerned about the welfare of children.

Roger Singleton
Senior Director, Barnardo's

An Overview

This report presents new evidence which shows that *relative* poverty has absolute effects and is a much more destructive social force than is generally recognised.

It focuses on the welfare of children and young people and discusses trends in health, depression, crime, drug abuse, suicides and educational standards. This report shows that the growth of relative poverty in Britain has had a major impact on the these trends.

The report's purpose is not to point a finger of blame at particular authorities or to suggest that childhood problems do not also have a host of other causes. It is, instead, to provide a clear demonstration that there is at least one important and remediable contributor to some of the social ills of our society.

Why, as society becomes more materially prosperous, are there increasing signs of social failure? This booklet shows that at least one major component of the answer is the scale of relative poverty and income inequality in society. Their social and psychological effects on the population have widespread repercussions.

No one doubts that economically deprived neighbourhoods suffer more than their share of poor health, crime, drug abuse, depression and other social problems. What this report adds is evidence from two new sources which show that the scale of these problems is responsive to changes in the extent of relative poverty over the years. First is new evidence from internationally comparable data on the distribution of personal income in different developed countries which allows the effects of income distribution to be compared between countries. Second, the unprecedented widening of income differences during the 1980s provides a new opportunity to assess the effects of changes in income distribution.

The damaging effects which disadvantage appears to have on the least well-off are, at most, only partly offset by the beneficial effects of increased advantage among the better-off. The issue is therefore not merely a matter of social justice: it is also a matter of overall national standards of attainment. The lower standards of health, of educational attainment, and the high cost of problems such as crime and drug use associated with increased relative poverty, are not only a human waste but an economic expense which a competitive modern economy cannot afford to accept. There is accumulating evidence that there is no trade-off-between equity and economic growth. Economic growth, productivity growth and investment are now higher in countries with smaller income differences. For the sake of the economy and society as a whole, as well as of young people themselves, we need greater investment in human capital.

While children's charities such as Barnardo's do their best to put young lives together, action to reduce relative poverty is a priority if we are to prevent them from being torn apart in the first place.

Richard G. Wilkinson

1. Introduction

It is tempting to let the eye skip over apparently dry statistics, but we cannot afford to ignore the trends in the list which follows. The figures all show adverse influences affecting children and young people during the 1980s. This period was chosen because the rapidity of change during that decade provides an opportunity to discover what lies behind them. As well as the unhappiness they record among children and young people, they affect the social fabric and the quality of life for all of us.

- Total reported crime, including juvenile crime, increased by almost 80 per cent and violent crime by 90 per cent during the ten years 1981–91.[1]
- The number of drug offenders between the ages of 17 and 29 doubled between 1979 and 1989.[2]
- There was between a four- and five-fold increase in the number of deaths from solvent abuse between 1980 and 1990.[3]
- The proportion of children on Child Protection Registers almost quadrupled during the 1980s. The rates of children 0 – 4 years old registered after sustaining serious injuries increased by 50 per cent between 1979 and 1989.[4]
- The number of children in care under the age of 10 increased from 1985 onwards.[5] The numbers under 4 years old increased by 30 per cent between 1986 and 1991.
- Reading standards among 7 – 8 year olds declined during the 1980s.[6]
- A study of school expulsions covering the period 1986 to 1991 reported dramatic increases in the use of "all types of exclusion for children in all age groups".[7]
- The suicide rate among young men aged 15 – 24 increased by 75 per cent from 1983 to reach a peak in 1990.[8]

There is no need to emphasise how worrying these trends are. The statistics represent only the visible tip of deeper social phenomena affecting the lives of a much larger proportion of children. The purpose of this report is to see what lies beneath them and how matters might be remedied.

Although some of the trends amalgamate changes in reporting with changes in what is really happening, not all do. Together they provide evidence of deteriorating social and psychological conditions among children and young people.

In a number of cases the changes reflect an acceleration of trends which have been going on for several decades. Rutter has suggested that there has been a long-term trend of rising psychiatric disorder and psychosocial problems among children and adolescents and that these include not only drug abuse, juvenile delinquency and suicide, but also depressive disorders, alcohol problems and anorexia.[9]

These problems should not be seen in isolation from each other. Instead of approaching them as half a dozen separate trends, as if they had only independent causes and just happened to coincide, this report starts out from the widely held view that we are dealing with a broadly based social malaise. That is to say that, as well as having many separate causes, the trends in crime, in suicides, drug abuse, depression and the increasing numbers of young children in care or on child abuse registers are also likely to have some important common causes.

Too often the reasons for such changes in the social fabric of society are treated as mysterious. Scientific investigation is inadequately resourced and its findings are often ignored. The result is that important aspects of children's lives, and of the quality of the social life of our society as a whole, continue to decline unchecked. If the increasing difficulties encountered by children and young people are to be tackled effectively, we must understand their underlying causes.

The simultaneous worsening in these social indicators provides a fresh incentive to investigate and try to understand what is going on. This report is prompted by two important developments which cast a powerful new light on what is happening. Both of them serve to clarify the contribution of changes in income distribution and relative poverty.

The first is that internationally comparable data on income distribution have recently become available covering a number of developed countries. As well as enabling comparisons to be made between countries at a given point in time, the new data also make it possible to look, in a limited number of societies, at the effects of changes in relative poverty over time. Suddenly we can begin to get a more objective view of the strains which a wider income distribution imposes on the fabric of a society.

The second development is that in the 1980s changes in income distribution in Britain became, for the first time, sufficiently rapid and substantial for researchers to be able to identify their social effects. Figure 1 shows the unprecedented widening of income differences during the 1980s. After slowly widening in the early 1980s, income differences widened very rapidly from 1985 onwards. The proportion of children living in households with incomes below half the national average (the definition of relative poverty chosen by the European Community) increased from 10 per cent in 1979, to 31 per cent in 1990/91 (after allowing for housing costs).[10] Such a sudden change allows its effects to be traced in detail for the first time. Previously income distribution had been too stable to identify its effects.

These developments have provided new evidence suggesting that income distribution and the extent of relative poverty have more important and more widespread effects than have yet been recognised. Most strikingly, national standards of health in the developed countries are, as we shall see, powerfully affected by how equal or unequal people's incomes are. So much so, that the best way of improving national standards of health in developed countries would almost certainly be by reducing income differences. It is much more important than, for instance, smoking or other behavioural risk factors.

Fig 1: Widening income differences

Distribution of disposable income adjusted for household size, UK.

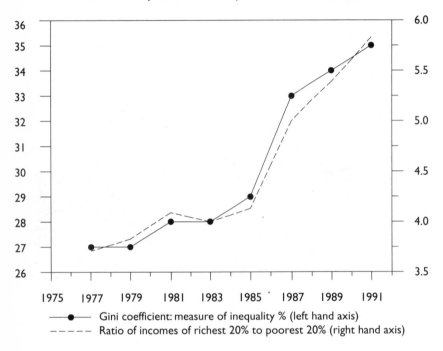

Gini coefficient: measure of inequality % (left hand axis)
Ratio of incomes of richest 20% to poorest 20% (right hand axis)

Fig 1 shows how income differences have widened in the UK since the late 1970s. Two different measures of inequality show the same pattern of a gradual widening of income differences which accelerated dramatically from 1984 or 1985. The Gini coefficient of inequality measures income differences, not simply between the rich and poor, but among the whole population. (The Gini coefficient can vary between 0 percent, which would mean everyone had exactly the same income, to 100 percent which would mean that one person had all the income and everyone else had none.) The other measure, shown here by the dotted line, records the growing disparity between the richest and poorest 20 percent of the population.

Fig 2: Indices showing changes in death rates among young adults, children and infants.

(Male and female combined, England and Wales 1975-92)

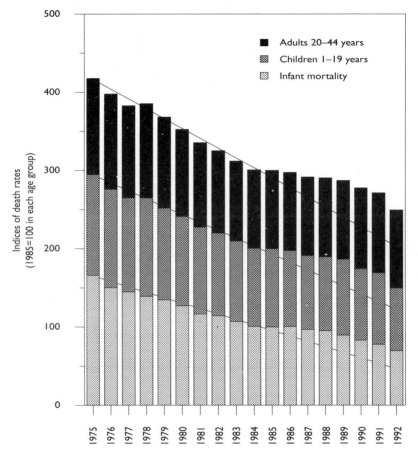

Fig 2 shows the trends in death rates among adults in the parental age range, children and infants. These are marked by the top, middle and bottom parts of the columns respectively. The death rates in each age group were set equal to 100 in 1985 so that the column for the three together came to 300 in 1985. The three diagonal lines project forward the downward trends which occurred prior to 1985. (They are fixed by the regression of death rates on the years 1975-84.) The point of the graph is to show that from 1985 (when income differences widened so dramatically) death rates in each group failed to fall nearly as fast as they had done prior to that date. The extra mortality resulting from the slow down in the decline is shown by the amount by which the columns rise above the diagonal trend lines.

Fig 3: The decline in reading standards

Chiltern reading test scores for all 7-8 year old
Buckinghamshire school children.

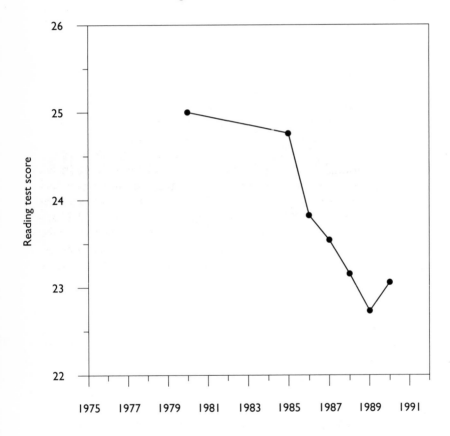

Fig 3 shows data from one of three studies which reported a decline in reading standards in primary schools from 1985. The scores are averages in each year for all 7-8 year olds in Buckinghamshire primary schools. There appears to have been a continuous, small - but statistically significant - decline in reading standards from 1985 to 1989.

The pathways through which income differences seem to affect health are likely to centre on just those social aspects of disadvantage which might be expected to lead to other expressions of social stress. Although the precise pathways are far from clear, it would appear that the scale of material differences in a society is a key determinant of the psychological and social well-being of a large part of the population. As such it has a corrosive effect on a society's social fabric and on the lives of its members. While it has always been known that poor school performance, higher crime rates and higher rates of a variety of other social problems are associated with greater relative deprivation, it is now possible to demonstrate – as this report will show – the worrying effects which widening differences in income have been having on children and young people.

An early indication of the strength of the links can be gained from Figures 1 – 3. They show that the dramatic widening of income differences from 1985 was accompanied by a marked slowing of the decline in national death rates for infants, children (and for adults below middle age – which includes most parents) and a simultaneous decline in reading standards among school children over the same years. Such coincidences reflect the way a wider dispersion of income inhibits, and may even retard educational and later career progress through restriction of parental resources, lower self-esteem and an increase in stress, family conflict and emotional disturbance in children – particularly among the growing numbers in relative poverty.

To concentrate on such predominantly psycho-social effects of increasing material inequality may seem to imply that absolute material need and poverty does not matter. Where it occurs it matters very much. The plight of the increasing numbers of homeless families and of young people reduced to begging demands the most urgent attention. Rather than playing down the less controversial effects of absolute deprivation, the intention is to show the importance of the effects of the much more widespread problems of relative deprivation. Extreme privation, such as malnutrition or exposure to cold, will of course have direct biological effects on people. But on top of these, there are also powerful social effects which are to a large extent related to social influences on identity, on self-respect and the processes of social differentiation and exclusion. Although strongest where deprivation is greatest, what this report will seek to show is that these processes have extremely powerful effects on our lives, not only beyond

the confines of anything which could be defined as absolute poverty, but
also beyond what is normally regarded as relative poverty. The message,
in a nutshell, is that the psycho-social concomitants of greater material
inequalities:

- damage physical health and the emotional welfare of a large
  proportion of the population;

- lead to changes in values and social behaviour;

- threaten a society's social and cultural cohesion.

Understanding the processes involved is central to any attempt to
understand the growing difficulties facing young people and families
bringing up children.

The difficulties of defining poverty, relative deprivation, disadvantage
or social exclusion, are not central to what follows. Most of the time it
is enough to say that the problems people encounter tend to increase the
further they are down the social scale. A sharp distinction is however
made between *absolute* and *relative* living standards. The absolute
standard of living relates purely to material conditions in which
people live. In contrast, the relative standard of living encompasses
inherently social processes: it involves a conception of where you are in
relation to others.

This report deals almost exclusively with the effects of widening
income differences on the lives of children and young people. For the
sake of clarity and brevity, little consideration has been given to the role
of other important personal resources such as education, savings,
property, social and family links, etc. Nor is there a discussion of
changes in health services, in education and transport policy although
these also play an important role. The central purpose is to establish the
links between the rapid widening of income differences in the UK
during the 1980s and the many adverse trends – such as those listed at
the start of this report – affecting children and young people.

A preliminary note on changing family structures

Before embarking on the discussion of the trends in income differentials
and their social effects, a word about the changes in family structure.
The growing number of lone parent families is often regarded as an
alternative explanation of the disturbing trends in the welfare of
children and young people. Although there was almost a three-fold

increase in the annual number of divorces during the 1970s, the figures then levelled off and there was little change during the 1980s.[11] The proportion of births outside marriage increased from 8 per cent in 1970, to 12 per cent in 1980, and then to 30 per cent in 1991.[12] However, the rise in the proportion of all births registered in either one name or in the names of both parents living at separate addresses (a better indication of the father's absence than whether a birth is outside marriage) increased from just under seven per cent in 1983 (when the figures first became available) to almost 14 per cent by 1991.[13] As a proportion of all families with dependent children, the proportion with a married or cohabiting couple has fallen from 92 per cent in 1971 to 81 per cent in 1991.[14] Looked at like this, the rise in lone parenthood is less dramatic than it first appeared to be. Nevertheless, there are now about two million children living in one parent families. Just over half of all lone parents were once married and are on their own as a result of divorce, separation or widowhood.

As explanations for the deterioration of aspects of the welfare of children and young people, the effects of changes in family structure and of the growth in relative poverty may seem hard to separate. For instance, poverty can lead to an increase in lone parent families as financial stress increases the risk of marital breakdown. Similarly, unemployment reduces the ability of young men to support a family. But because lone parent families are usually relatively poor, an increase in their numbers tends, in turn, to increase the proportion of the population in relative poverty. In addition, changes in relative poverty and in family structure are both likely to contribute towards changing values and culture. However, research workers have managed to disentangle some of the separate influences of the two.

One important indicator is that much of the association between lone parenting and less good intellectual and educational performance of children seems to be related to poverty rather than to lone parenthood itself. The children of lone parents have more signs of emotional disturbance and do less well educationally. But these disadvantages do not flow automatically from having only one parent. Because environmental factors which are known to affect children's development, such as low social class, poor housing and low incomes, occur much more frequently among lone parent families it is important to separate out the effects of being brought up by only one parent from the socioeconomic disadvantages which so often go with it. At any one time some 70 per cent of lone parents are receiving Income Support to alleviate their poverty, and a higher proportion need it at some time while their children are still dependants.[14]

Data from child development studies show that almost all the deficits suffered by children brought up by single parents are accounted for by their socioeconomic disadvantage.[15] [16] When indicators of emotional disturbance and educational performance are compared, apart from children of divorced or separated parents, the children of better off lone parents do as well as the children in better off two-parent families, and poorer children of lone parents do as well as the poorer children with both parents.[15] Children of divorced or separated parents do show significant developmental disadvantages, but the indications from large follow-up studies are that these disadvantages start before couples separate and reflect the emotional effects of the domestic conflict which lead to the separation.[17] [18] However, results from a smaller retrospective case-control study expected soon are likely to dispute the extent to which later disadvantage is attributable largely to earlier domestic conflict rather than to some additional effects of parental separation and divorce. Parents contemplating divorce must inevitably have an agonising decision weighing the likely damage caused by divorce against that which would be caused by prolonging domestic conflict. A thorough review of the evidence on the effects on children of lone parenthood and family disruption has recently been published by the Family Policy Studies Centre.[19]

The possibility of overcoming the handicapping effects of poverty associated with lone-parent families can be seen through international comparisons. Among developed countries, Japan and Sweden represent the opposite ends of the spectrum of family structures. Japan remains closest to the two-parent nuclear family model, with very few births outside marriage and low divorce rates, while Sweden – with over half its births outside marriage – is surpassed only by Iceland in the extent of its departure from this pattern.[20] But, despite such a stark contrast, they do almost equally well in terms of child welfare and health. They come first and second in the international league table of life expectancy at birth and have low crime rates. That such major differences in family structure should produce such small differences in outcome is, this paper will argue, a reflection of the fact that these two countries have the narrowest income differences in the developed world. During the last generation, Japanese income differences have narrowed dramatically to become smaller than in Sweden. In Sweden, the celebrated support provided for parents ensured that in 1987, after taxes and benefits, only two per cent of Swedish children in lone parent families were in relative poverty compared with an average of 21.2 per cent for a group of eight countries in the Organisation for Economic Co-operation and Development (OECD).[21] Among children living with both parents, only 1.5 per cent were in relative poverty in Sweden compared with an average of 5.7 per cent for other countries. Partly as a result, infant mortality rates for illegitimate babies in Sweden are as low as those for legitimate births in social classes I and II in England and Wales (see Figure 4).[22]

Fig 4: Social class differences in infant mortality in Sweden compared to England and Wales.

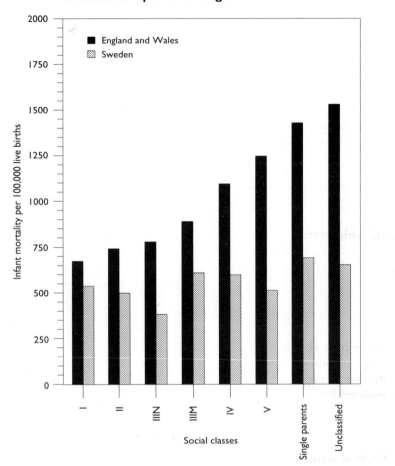

Fig 4 contrasts the steep social class gradient in infant mortality in England and Wales (the taller black bars) with less systematic differences in Sweden (the shorter grey bars) where income differences are much smaller. Not only is there no consistent gradient in infant mortality across these groups in Sweden, but death rates are lower in almost all the Swedish groups than the lowest in England and Wales. (Social classes are based on occupations: professionals in social class I down to unskilled manual occupations in social class V. Social class III is divided between IIIN, containing junior non-manual occupations - such as clerical workers, and IIIM containing skilled manual occupations.)

2. The Effect of Income Distribution on Health — International Evidence

Although internationally comparable data on income distribution has recently become available from the Luxembourg Income Study, there are rather few *internationally* comparable measures of things that might be affected by it. Crime rates and most measures of children's welfare are too influenced by differences in definition and in reporting systems to make valid comparisons. Death rates, however, are an exception. Indeed, they provide the clearest evidence that changes in relative income have absolute effects.

This section outlines the evidence showing that national mortality rates are strongly influenced by the extent of *relative* deprivation (as measured by income distribution) in each society. This is an important point at which to start an analysis of the psychosocial malaise because it is – as we shall see – through psychological and social pathways that income distribution affects mortality. Having shown the power of the effects of income differences on these "hard" data, we shall then go on, in subsequent sections, to outline changes in other aspects of the welfare of children and young people during the 1980s. The report ends with a discussion of the processes which link wider income differences to their social effects.

Work on the effect of income on health developed as part of an attempt to explain the social class differences in death rates found within developed countries. In Britain in recent decades unskilled manual workers and their families have been found to have death rates two or three times as high as the death rates among people in professional occupations and their families.[23] This means that for people of a given age in each social class, two or three times the proportion will die each year in lower as in upper classes. Differences such as these occur at most ages and extend to most causes of death. They are not caused by differences in medical care. Not only are differences in access to medical care small, but medical care is not one of the major influences on the main causes of death in the developed world.[24] Similarly, lifestyle differences such as smoking, diet and exercise,[25] and the tendency for the unhealthy to move down the social hierarchy[26 27] leave most of the health differences unexplained.

There is a great deal of evidence showing that measures of health within countries are related to almost any measure of socioeconomic deprivation – including car ownership, education and whether people own or rent their homes.[23] For example, Figure 5 shows the clear gradient of declining mortality rates as one goes up the income scale in the USA.

Fig 5: Income and mortality among white US men

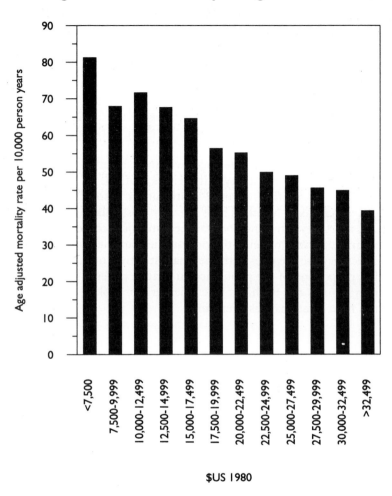

Source: MRFIT data from Davey Smith G, Neaton J D, and Stamler J.
Income differentials in mortality risk among 305,099 white men. 1994 (forthcoming).

Fig 5 illustrates the remarkably regular relationship between death rates and indicators of social and economic status of people within most developed countries. This data, from a particularly large American study, shows how death rates of white men decline with increasing income.

However, it is important to recognise that the size of these social class differences in death rates is neither fixed nor unalterable. It differs substantially from one country to another and from one historical period to the next. In Britain the evidence covering most of the present century suggests that the size of the social class differences in death rates has got larger or smaller as the proportion of the population living in relative poverty has increased or decreased.[28] The same relationship between differences in income and in mortality is also suggested by international evidence showing that member countries of the OECD with larger income differences tend to be those with larger mortality differences.[29]

But the scale of income differences within a society does more than affect the scale of mortality differences within it. International comparisons show that income distribution also affects *average* national standards of health. There is a very close relationship between national mortality rates and societal measures of income dispersion in each country. Instead of being the richest, the countries with the longest life expectancy are the ones with the smallest spread of incomes and the smallest proportion of the population in relative poverty.[30] [31] As we shall see from Figures 6 – 9, this is true whether you look at countries at a point in time or at changes over time.

Fig 6: Life expectancy (M & F) and Gini coefficients of post-tax income inequality (standardised for household size)

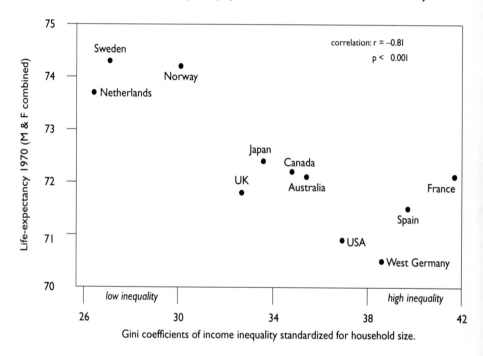

Gini coefficients of income inequality standardized for household size.

Sources: Data from Sawyer M, Income distribution in OECD countries, *OECD Economic Outlook,*
Occasional Studies, 1976, 3–36, Table 11; and World Bank

Fig 6 uses the earliest comparable data available to show that the countries with the highest average life expectancy (at birth for men and women combined) were those like Sweden, Norway and the Netherlands where income differences within each country were smaller. Less egalitarian countries, like France, Spain, West Germany and the USA, had life expectancies about three years lower. The striking contrast between the more recent experience of Britain and Japan is discussed in the text. A note on the Gini coefficient of inequality is included in the note on figure 2.

Fig 7: The annual rate of change of life expectancy in 12 European Community countries and the rate of change in the percentage of the population in relative poverty 1975-85

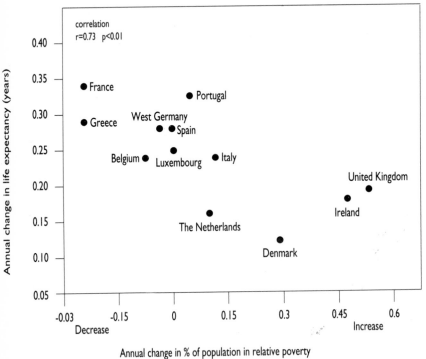

Annual change in % of population in relative poverty

Source: Data from O'Higgins M and Jenkins S P, Poverty in the EC. In: Teekens R, van Praag B M S (eds)
Analysing poverty in the European Community, Luxembourg, EUROSTAT,1990.

Fig 7 shows that the rate of improvement in life expectancy in European countries was related to changes in the extent of relative poverty. The horizontal axis shows whether the proportion of the population living on less than half the average income in each country was increasing or decreasing 1975–85. The vertical axis shows how fast average life expectancy increased in each country over the same period. Both are expressed as an average annual amount of change.

Using a standard measure of income distribution, Figure 6 shows that in 1970 the countries with the smallest income differences were also the countries where average life expectancy was longest. In the years since then the rate of growth of average life expectancy has been closely related to changes in income distribution.[30] Figure 7 shows that in the 12 member states of the European Community average life expectancy has grown fastest in those countries where relative poverty decreased fastest (or increased slowest) between 1975 and 1985. Data from a different source – which includes a number of countries outside the EC – is illustrated in Figure 8 which again shows that the fastest increases in life expectancy have occurred in countries where income differences have narrowed. (It is worth noting that the effect of widening income distribution in these examples is to slow down rather than reverse the long-term decline in mortality rates.) Lastly, Figure 9 shows a cross-sectional relationship between the prevalence of relative poverty in different countries and *infant* mortality rates.

Fig 8: Changes in income distribution and life expectancy in different countries over 5-10 year periods

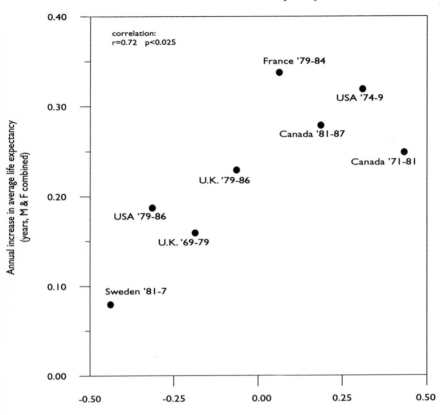

Annual change in % share of disposable income
received by least well-off 50% (adjusted for household size)

Source: Data from the Luxembourg Income Study database

Fig 8, like figure 7, shows that countries in which income differences have diminished have enjoyed faster increases in average life expectancy than have those in which the income gap between rich and poor has widened. The horizontal axis shows the increase or decrease in the share of societal income going to the poorest half of the population. The countries on the left experienced widening income differences (albeit from very different starting points) while those to the right experienced a narrowing of income differences during the periods shown. The vertical axis shows how fast life expectancy has improved. As in figure 7, both axes show annual rates of change.

Fig 9: Relative poverty and infant mortality rate for nine OECD countries 1980

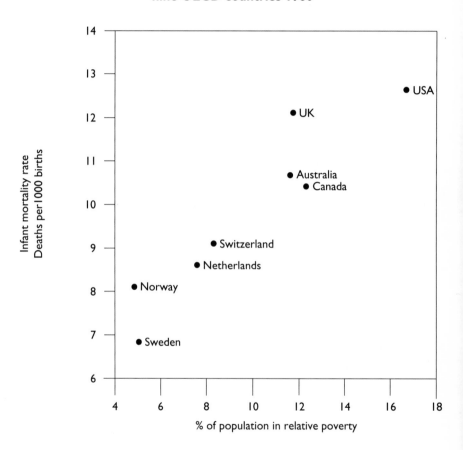

Source: Wennemo I, *Sociology of health and illness* 1993; 15: 429–46

Fig 9 shows that the countries with the highest infant mortality rates (higher on the vertical axis) tend to be those where the proportion of the population in relative poverty was greatest (to the right on the horizontal axis).

Despite the small number of countries for which there are comparable data, the relationships with measures of income distribution shown in Figures 6 – 9 are all statistically significant. Nor do statistical controls suggest that these relationships can be explained as expressions of underlying factors such as better public services in more egalitarian societies. The relationship implies that between a half and three-quarters of the differences in average life expectancy between one developed country and another may be attributable to differences in income distribution alone.

A telling example of the influence of income distribution on health is the contrast between health trends in Britain and Japan. Figure 6 shows that in 1970 life expectancy and income distribution were quite similar in both countries. Since then Japan's income distribution has narrowed to become the narrowest of any country reporting to the World Bank. At the same time life expectancy in Japan has increased by 6.9 years in the period 1970 – 90 and is now the highest in the world. In contrast Britain's income distribution has widened and Britain's position in the life expectancy league table of OECD countries has fallen from 10th in 1970 to 17th in 1990 with a gain of only 3.9 years in life expectancy. Although Britain has enjoyed some of the general increase in life expectancy, the widening of income differences just to 1986 appears to have slowed down the increase enough to deprive the average citizen of an additional year's life expectancy which the data suggests would have been gained had income distribution not widened.[32]

The powerful influence of the contrasting trends in income distribution in the two countries is confirmed by what has been happening to their social class mortality differences. As Japanese income differences have narrowed so too have their social class differences in death rates.[33] In Britain, both income and mortality differences have widened.[34] It is these divergent trends in inequalities which lie behind the contrasting gains in average life expectancy.

Fig 10: Increases in life expectancy and increases in GDP per capita in OECD countries 1970-90

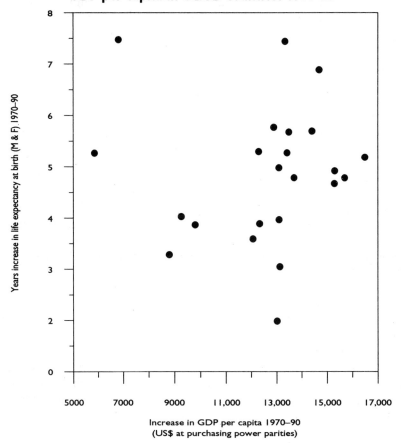

Source: OECD *National Accounts*, Paris, 1992 and World Bank, *World Tables*, 1992

Fig 10 shows that during the 20 years 1970-90 there was no clear relationship between economic growth and increases in life expectancy. Economic growth is expressed on the horizontal axis in terms of the amount of increase in Gross Domestic Product per capita, while the vertical axis shows the years added to life expectancy in the same 20-year period. National currencies are converted into dollars according to their real purchasing power in each country so that the horizontal axis expresses increases in average real incomes. The lack of any clear relationship in this graph contrasts sharply with the relationships with income levels within a country shown in figure 5, and with the distribution of income in figures 6-9. These contrasts suggest that in developed countries death rates are affected more by relative than absolute income levels.

WITHIN COUNTRIES MORTALITY RATES ARE CLOSELY ASSOCIATED WITH PEOPLE'S SOCIAL AND ECONOMIC CIRCUMSTANCES. BUT WHEN COMPARISONS ARE MADE BETWEEN DEVELOPED COUNTRIES THEY SHOW THAT AVERAGE LIFE EXPECTANCY IS NOT RELATED TO A COUNTRY'S AVERAGE WEALTH.

THE APPARENT PARADOX ARISES BECAUSE HEALTH IS AFFECTED MORE BY RELATIVE THAN BY ABSOLUTE INCOME LEVELS. THIS IS CONFIRMED BY THE CLOSE RELATIONSHIP BETWEEN INCOME DISTRIBUTION AND NATIONAL MORTALITY RATES.

NOT ONLY IS LIFE EXPECTANCY LONGEST IN COUNTRIES WHERE INCOME DIFFERENCES ARE SMALLEST, BUT THE DATA SHOWS THAT CHANGES IN INCOME DISTRIBUTION AFFECT THE RATE OF CHANGE IN LIFE EXPECTANCY.

3. Trends in the UK during the 1980s

Figure 1 shows that income differences in the UK widened gradually until 1984 or 1985 when they suddenly started to widen very dramatically. The mid and later 1980s stand out as having the most rapid widening of differentials for which we have reliable measures. It therefore provides a unique opportunity to assess the effects of income distribution on various aspects of people's lives. If it significantly increased the pressures on families we might expect it to have left its mark on indicators of health and welfare. Before analysing the extent to which some of the adverse trends in the welfare of young people during the 1980s may have arisen from this source, we shall first look to see what effect the rapid widening of income differentials had on death rates.

Health

As the international data discussed above make clear, health – as measured by death rates – shows a long-term tendency to improve at all ages. The background rate of improvement does not seem to be explained by economic growth or by advances in medical care: indeed its causes are largely unknown. We have also seen that a wider income distribution slows down the national decline in mortality rates. However, changes in income distribution are generally too slight to halt the decline in death rates.

It is of concern, therefore, that in his annual report for 1990, the Chief Medical Officer at the Department of Health drew attention to what, on his initial data, appeared to be a rise in national mortality rates for men and women aged 15 – 44 years which started in 1985.[36] The changes in death rates for young adults, children and infants are shown in Figure 2. This shows that the decline in death rates in each of these age groups slowed down from 1985. The diagonal lines between the columns show how much lower the death rates would have been if the rate of decline during the period 1975-84 had been maintained after 1985.

The Chief Medical Officer said that the trend in death rates in the 15-44 age group could not be explained by AIDS deaths. Since then it has been suggested that deaths from opportunistic causes associated with, but not attributed to, AIDS might account for the figures.[37] There are two problems with that. First, even the generous allowance suggested for hidden AIDS deaths is not enough to account fully for the departure from the earlier trend. The second problem is that we can now see much the same pattern in the infants' and children's death rates which are also shown in Figure 2: their rate of decline slowed over the same years. The temporary levelling off in the mortality decline during the later 1980s is visible in infant mortality and in each five-year age group up to the age of 20 years. However, there were only 47 deaths from AIDS among all children up to 15 years old from the start of the epidemic up to July 1992.[38] So if AIDS cannot be the explanation among children, and cannot account for all the slowing of the decline in mortality rates in the other age groups, another explanation is needed.

Not only are there notable increases in deaths attributable to suicide and alcohol, which are plausibly related to the effects of increasing relative deprivation, but there is also evidence that the adverse trends in mortality occur in the most deprived parts of Britain. There are two pieces of evidence on this.

Fig 11: Standardised mortality ratios (SMRs) for Greater Glasgow Health Board 0-64 year age group, M & F, all causes

(Scotland=100)

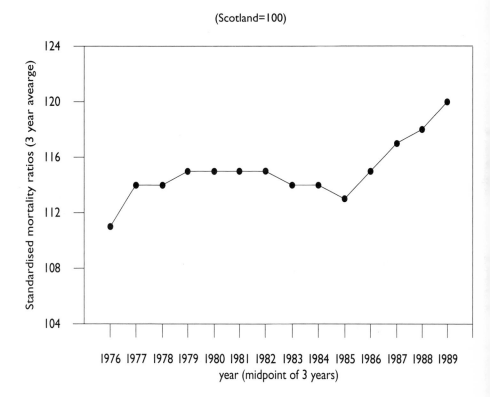

Source: Annual Report of the Director of Public Health, Greater Glasgow Health Board, 1991/92.

Fig 11 shows on the vertical axis how age-standardised death rates in Glasgow compared with those for Scotland as a whole (set equal to 100). Until 1985, Glasgow's death rates - at about 114 or 115 - were 14 or 15 percent higher than Scotland's. After 1985 Glasgow's mortality disadvantage increased steadily. The significance of this is that Glasgow is the most deprived area of Scotland and its mortality disadvantage increased during the years in which income differences widened nationally.

The first comes from Glasgow which includes some of the most deprived parts of Scotland. Figure 11 shows the death rates of men and women 0 – 64 years in the Greater Glasgow Health Board area compared with the rest of Scotland (set equal to 100). The standardised mortality ratios (SMRs) show that, although death rates in Glasgow were higher than the Scottish average in the late 1970s and early 1980s, they were fairly stable in relation to the rest of Scotland. In 1985 they were about 13 per cent above that for Scotland as a whole. The disparity then increased steadily until, in 1989, death rates were over 20 per cent higher than for Scotland. In his annual report for 1991/92, the Director of Public Health for the Greater Glasgow Health Board reported on a statistical analysis of area differences in mortality rates and said "deprivation alone therefore accounts for almost 80 per cent of the relatively high mortality in the Greater Glasgow Health Board Population" under 65 years old.[39]

The second piece of evidence relating the adverse trend in mortality to relative deprivation comes from an analysis of small area statistics in the north of England.[40] Comparable measures of deprivation for each of the 678 electoral wards of the Northern Region of England were taken from the 1981 and 1991 censuses and related to age-specific mortality rates for five different age groups between 0 and 74 years. The authors found a widening of social and economic differences between the wards over the decade that was accompanied by a widening of mortality differences. In the poorest wards mortality levels at some ages had risen during the decade. Among the less poor there was little change, while among the better off they had continued to decline.

Mortality trends in Glasgow and in the Northern Region of England both show adverse effects associated with relative deprivation. In the Northern region we know that the trends are associated with increasing relative deprivation and in Glasgow we know that the timing exactly fits the timing of the national increases in relative deprivation. This pattern of changing mortality is very much what would be expected in the light of the international evidence of the effects of income distribution on mortality discussed earlier.

As well as substantial international evidence that increases in relative deprivation adversely affect national mortality rates, we have also seen that the rapid increases in relative deprivation after 1985 affected national mortality rates among children and adults below 45 years old. We shall now go on to look at other aspects of the welfare of young people which might show the marks of widening income differences during the 1980s.

FROM THE MID 1980S THERE WAS A SLOW DOWN IN THE RATE OF DECLINE IN NATIONAL MORTALITY RATES FOR INFANTS, CHILDREN AND YOUNG ADULTS. AS WELL AS COINCIDING WITH THE WIDENING OF INCOME DIFFERENCES, THE SLOW DOWN REFLECTS MORTALITY TRENDS IN DEPRIVED AREAS.

MORTALITY RATES BETWEEN RICH AND POOR WARDS IN THE NORTHERN REGION WIDENED BETWEN 1981 AND 1991 AS RELATIVE DEPRIVATION INCREASED.

THE EXCESS MORTALITY ASSOCIATED WITH GLASGOW'S DEPRIVATION RELATIVE TO THE REST OF SCOTLAND INCREASED FROM THE MID 1980S.

Declining reading standards

Unlike mortality, data on many other areas of human activity are heavily influenced by changes in reporting and in administrative criteria. This makes it much harder to get an accurate idea of the real changes in society. We shall start this section with a discussion of data on children's reading scores because, instead of being affected by trends in reporting as are figures on child abuse, drugs or crime, some schools and Local Education Authorities administer reading tests systematically to all children each year. The average scores then provide a reasonably accurate guide to changing standards.

The first report of a decline in reading standards came from an anonymous group of educational psychologists who said that standards had declined in eight of the LEAs in which they worked during the 1980s "and in particular during the period since 1985". This report prompted further research. The National Foundation for Educational Research (NFER) was commissioned by the School Examinations and Assessment Council to review evidence of changes in reading standards of 7 year olds during the 1980s. It undertook two pieces of research. The first simply involved collecting records from LEAs. Of the 26 with records which co-operated, they found evidence of a decline in reading standards among 19. They stated that "The trend that was reflected in the results provided by the LEAs emerged most clearly after 1985."[41]

Because of possible weaknesses in the data, they took another random sample of schools and examined changes over the period between 1987, when new tests were introduced, and 1991. Their findings confirmed the decline. Although the government of the day had originally attributed the decline to the use of the so-called "real books" method of teaching reading, "no significant associations were found ... between the [teaching] methods used and pupils' reading performance".

The lack of connection between declining reading standards and teaching methods was underscored by Croydon Education Authority which reported that "in the period 1986/87 to 1989/90 mathematics performance had declined comparably to the decline evident in reading".[42] The NFER pointed out that "in the majority of cases where the [reading] decline was apparent, this seemed to relate to an increase in the percentage of pupils in the lowest-scoring groups rather than an all-round decline". In terms of social geography, *none* of the few schools which showed a rise in reading performance was an inner-city school or in an area generally associated with need or disadvantage. In contrast, half of those where standards fell were in large conurbations and industrial centres.

Methodologically the best study was conducted by a senior educational psychologist in Buckinghamshire Education Authority who was able to analyse the results of the same reading test which had been administered throughout the county each year during the 1980s. The decline in average reading scores across the county as a whole were shown in Figure 3 earlier in this report. The author says "1985 is clearly a watershed year, as suggested also in Turner's data."[43] In terms of an explanation he also found no evidence that the suspect teaching methods were to blame. Instead he found that the schools where the decline happened were schools with the poorest catchment areas. This was the only reliable correlate of the decline. Deteriorating standards in these areas more than offset the small gains in some more prosperous areas. The suggestion that deprived home backgrounds were the problem was strengthened by the results of other tests designed to measure the kind of general knowledge which children might expect to get from their home background rather than from school. The results showed "deterioration in the quality of background experiences of the less able readers – who also . . . tend to come from the less privileged areas".

We have then clear evidence of a decline in average reading standards unexplained by teaching methods. It appears to have been the result of declining standards among the less good readers attending schools in the more deprived areas. Its timing is almost identical to the timing of the rapid increase in relative deprivation and with the point at which the mortality of parents and children ceased its downward trend.

The proportion of children living in relative poverty increased three-fold during the 1980s. Almost a third of the children in the average classroom now come from homes below the EC relative income poverty line (households with less than half the national average income). As that proportion increases it is to be expected that both teaching and learning become more difficult. The deleterious effect of deprivation on educational performance is well known. Indeed the relationship was the rationale for the recent report *Access and Achievement in Urban Education* from the Office for Standards in Education.[44] The correlation coefficient between the proportion of children in LEAs getting five or more GCSE passes with grades A – C in 1991/92 and the Department of the Environment's summary index of each area's social deprivation is 0.81, implying that two-thirds of the variations in GCSE performance between LEAs is related to social deprivation.[45]

A particularly striking illustration of the way in which poor educational performance and ill health are expressions of the effects of relative deprivation comes from the National Child Development Study which has followed up 17,000 people born in 1958. It found that the best predictor of their health at age 23 was teachers' assessment of their behaviour when they were 16 years old. Those identified by teachers using the Rutter Behaviour Scale as showing "deviant" behaviour – "emotional or conduct disorders" – scored much less well on the health measures at age 23, even after taking many other social and economic factors into account.[46] That deviance is related to health even when it is not associated with socioeconomic disadvantage does not of course mean that most deviance is unrelated to disadvantage. Indeed, the 1958 cohort study shows clearly that socioeconomic disadvantage is an important factor predisposing to deviance. The finding is interesting because it gives a glimpse of the extent to which educational, behavioural and health problems have to be seen as intimately related and sharing causes.

Evidence that increases or decreases in deprivation will produce corresponding changes in educational performance is not confined to the striking relationship we have seen between declining reading standards and increasing relative deprivation during the 1980s. There are signs that the international data on educational performance echoes the relationship of mortality data to income distribution. Thus, although British children's maths scores are closely related to their parents' occupational class, in Japan, where income differences have become much smaller, there is evidence to suggest that they may not be. Some of the questions in the third International Math Test showed no differences according to father's occupation in the proportion of Japanese 11-year-old children giving correct answers.[47]

There is also impressive evidence of an interaction between relative deprivation and the specific effect which low birthweight has in depressing children's IQ scores. In a follow-up study which matched low birthweight babies (<2500g) with controls according to parental characteristics including social class, it was found that the intellectual impairment associated with low birthweight disappeared among the non-manual social classes.[48] Children at the age of 10 who had been low birthweight babies did less well than their matched controls only among manual social classes. In contrast, low birthweight babies with more advantaged backgrounds did as well as their controls from the same backgrounds on both the verbal and performance scales of the WISC intelligence tests at age 10.

One might expect that the connection between increased relative deprivation and poorer educational performance would show up in an increasing proportion of children with "statements of special education-al need" or learning difficulties. But this is not so. A joint report from the Audit Commission and Her Majesty's Inspectorate of Schools says first, that "There is evidence to show that the level of deprivation in an area is an indicator of the incidence of special educational need." It then goes on to point out that "the likelihood of a child getting a statement depends more on the LEA's interpretation of the 1981 Act than it does on the proportion of pupils with special needs in the LEA".[49] Thus for purely administrative reasons "there is no correlation between the proportion of pupils with a statement and the level of deprivation in the study LEAs".

> **THERE HAS BEEN A THREE-FOLD INCREASE IN CHILDREN LIVING BELOW THE EC RELATIVE INCOME POVERTY LINE DURING THE 1980S. SUCH CHILDREN NOW MAKE UP ALMOST A THIRD OF THE AVERAGE CLASSROOM.**
>
> **AS RELATIVE POVERTY HAS INCREASED, READING STANDARDS HAVE FALLEN. THE DECLINE IN STANDARDS IS UNRELATED TO TEACHING METHODS AND TOOK PLACE IN DEPRIVED AREAS DURING THE YEARS WHEN RELATIVE DEPRIVATION INCREASED MOST RAPIDLY.**
>
> **THERE IS EVIDENCE TO SUGGEST THAT HEALTH AND EDUCATIONAL PERFORMANCE ARE AFFECTED BY RELATIVE DEPRIVATION THROUGH SIMILAR PSYCHO-SOCIAL CHANNELS.**

Welfare

There are numerous indications of a rapid growth in problems associated with social disadvantage among children in the later 1980s. The proportion of children placed on Child Protection Registers is likely to be influenced by changes in administrative guidelines and major news stories which have brought child abuse into the media – though both of these are themselves partly responses to the perceived problem. Nevertheless, the rate per 1000 of children 0 – 14 years placed on Child Protection Registers rose slowly from the later 1970s and then very rapidly in the years 1984 – 89.[4] Indicating that these trends are at least partly a reflection of a real increase in problems, the later 1980s saw higher rates of children 0 – 4 who were fatally or seriously injured. From 1985 there was also an increase in the proportion of children under 10 years old taken into care. The three factors which have been consistently most frequently stated, case by case on registration forms, as the main factors contributing to child abuse were "marital problems", "debts" and "unemployment".[4]

The number of children expelled from school has also increased rapidly. Comparable statistics are available only from 1986, but a survey of 78 LEAs conducted by the Advisory Centre for Education (ACE) showed that there had been a rapid and accelerating growth in expulsions from both primary and secondary schools during the period 1986—91.[50] There were plausible reasons for thinking that this may have been partly related to changes in the school system, particularly to the introduction of the Local Management of Schools policy. However, the ACE study found no correlation between the rate at which LEAs delegated their powers to individual schools and the rate at which expulsions increased.

Most commentators believe that there has been a contribution from an increase in the number of children with behavioural problems, and the OFSTED report, *Education for Disaffected Pupils* lists "increased stress in families being reflected in difficult behaviour in schools" as the first of the possible explanations.[51] Research which asked LEAs about changes in the proportions of significantly disturbed behaviour in schools found that 40 of the 52 which replied said it had increased, while only one said it had decreased.[52] It has been suggested that there may also be a lower tolerance of disturbed children.[53]

The proportion of children with difficulties which might be related to school expulsion is high and closely influenced by levels of relative deprivation. Estimates suggest that 10 per cent of children, rising to 20 per cent of adolescents, suffer from either "emotional disorders" – such as persistent fears, anxiety states, phobias and psychosomatic disorders – or "conduct disorders" including stealing, truancy, aggression, fire setting and more persistent delinquency.[54] In the Inner London Education Authority it was estimated that some 20 per cent of children were "poorly adjusted" in 1986. The same rating scale used in two schools more recently has produced much higher estimates.[43]

Among older children and adolescents there are also clear signs of the social costs of increased relative deprivation. They are found in the statistics and reports on drug related offences and deaths, suicides, child prostitution, teenage pregnancies and in criminal statistics.

ALONGSIDE THE WIDENING INCOME DIFFERENTIALS OF THE LATE 1980S THE FOLLOWING RATES HAVE ALL INCREASED:

- **0 – 14 YEAR OLDS PLACED ON CHILD PROTECTION REGISTERS;**

- **0 – 4 YEAR OLDS FATALLY OR SERIOUSLY INJURED;**

- **0 – 10 YEAR OLDS TAKEN INTO CARE;**

- **EXPULSIONS FROM PRIMARY AND SECONDARY SCHOOLS;**

THESE TRENDS ARE CONSISTENT WITH INCREASED STRESSES ON FAMILY LIFE RESULTING FROM GROWING RELATIVE POVERTY.

Homelessness

Homelessness is a rather different issue from the trends in education, health and welfare which we have discussed. While those record the human responses to increased relative deprivation, the rise in homelessness is a direct expression of the underlying problem of increasing deprivation itself. However, it is a particularly important expression because it deepens people's deprivation so fundamentally. The statistics on homelessness are statistics of the destruction of the material basis of normal life from which it is difficult to recover. Homelessness means acute social stress, family disruption and desperation – with all the social and psychological "knock-on" effects that sets in train. It is thus especially worrying to note the sharp increases in homelessness in the late 1980s.

Between 1985 and 1990 the number of *households* accepted as homeless by local authorities in England increased by 75 per cent.[55] Between 1986 and 1990 the total number of households in the UK accepted as in priority need under the homelessness legislation increased by almost 40 per cent to 155,700, and the total living in temporary accommodation more than doubled.[2] The number of homes repossessed by building societies increased 15 times from 4870 in 1981 to reach a peak of 75,540 in 1991.[56] At that date there were also some 275,000 homes at least six months in arrears on mortgage payments.

To the number of homeless households must be added the "hidden homeless". In 1988 benefit rates were reduced for 18 – 24 year olds and general entitlement to Income Support was removed from most unemployed 16 and 17 year olds. People aged 16 and 17 who are living away from home for a "good reason" (e.g. because their health would be at risk at home) are eligible for Income Support at the lower (18 – 24 year old) rate. Those who have left a job or Youth Training place can receive an allowance of £15 a week for up to eight weeks in a year. Apart from this, most of this age group, even if they are living away from their parents, receive benefits on a discretionary basis only if they complete a complicated claims procedure and are judged to be at risk of "severe hardship". There were 76,957 such claims in the first nine months of 1992. Most 16 and 17 year olds who are not in work, training or education receive nothing at all.[57]

Three years after these changes the Government commissioned a survey of 16 and 17 year olds who had claimed special hardship payments. It found that 45 per cent had been forced to sleep "rough" at some point, many were still homeless, half had no money, and a quarter of them said they had needed to beg, steal or sell drugs in order to survive. A quarter already had criminal convictions, and a quarter of the girls were pregnant.[58] Almost two-thirds of those not living at home had been thrown out and over 20 per cent said they had been physically or sexually abused while at home.

Pressures from a variety of sources coupled with almost a standstill in house building, meant that estimates of the numbers of homeless *people* (including estimates for the hidden homeless) reached about 700,000 in 1990.[59]

OVER ONE IN A HUNDRED PEOPLE IN THE UK ARE HOMELESS.

ALONGSIDE THE WIDENING INCOME DIFFERENTIALS OF THE LATE 1980s:

■ **THE NUMBERS OF PEOPLE IN PRIORITY NEED FOR HOUSING AND THOSE IN TEMPORARY ACCOMMODATION SHARPLY INCREASED;**

■ **BUILDING SOCIETY REPOSSESSIONS SOARED.**

OF THE TENS OF THOUSANDS OF UNEMPLOYED 16 AND 17 YEAR OLDS MAKING CLAIMS FOR DISCRETIONARY SEVERE HARDSHIP PAYMENTS, 45% HAD BEEN FORCED AT SOME TIME TO SLEEP ROUGH.

Suicide

For some time men's and women's suicide rates have been diverging. Women's rates have been lower and declining while men's have risen. However, what is striking about the trends during the 1980s is that the suicide rates for young men 15 – 24 years old start to rise very rapidly from about 1983 or 1984. The trends for young men and women are shown in Figure 12. Although the trends in each sex continue to be very different, there is more than a suggestion that the substantial decline in women's rates shown before 1984 was then halted and possibly reversed. So although women were largely protected from the increase in suicides among men, the same influences are just visible.

It might be thought that the timing of the rising suicide rate among young men fits in well enough with the trends in income distribution. But the fact that suicides start to rise a year or so earlier than the most rapid increase in relative deprivation needs some explanation. There seem to have been three contributory factors. One is that almost every year from 1982 to 1988 changes were made to restrict both entitlement to benefit among young people and the amount payable.[60][61] Secondly, unemployment rose earlier among the young to reach a peak in the mid 1980s before falling to a low in 1990. Suicides in Britain are known to be closely related to the trends in and distribution of unemployment.[62] Lastly the earnings of young people in employment fell relative to adults during the early 1980s to reach a low in 1984.[63]

But why have young women's suicide rates not shown the same dramatic rise? Although women's health and welfare is no less affected by environmental factors, there are three important differences. The first is that more women have entered the labour market. Although the proportion registered as unemployed has also increased, there has also been a rise in the proportion with paid jobs. However, employment among young men has declined and the loss of the traditional "bread-winner" role has undermined self-esteem and left a gap which is hard to fill. Secondly, the birth rate to women under 20 declined during the early 1980s and then rose from 1985. The presence of a child is protective against suicide.[64] Thirdly, the proportion of live births to women under 20 registered only in the mothers' name or in the joint names of parents living at different addresses rose from 29 per cent in 1983 to 52 per cent in 1991.[13] This means that more women than men had family links to protect against suicide.

SUICIDE RATES AMONG YOUNG MEN ROSE RAPIDLY IN THE MID TO LATE 1980S. THE EARLIER ONSET OF THE RISE THAN THE OTHER TRENDS CONSIDERED HERE MATCHES THE TIMING OF RESTRICTIONS TO BENEFIT ENTITLEMENT, UNEMPLOYMENT AMONG YOUNG PEOPLE AND LOWER RELATIVE EARNINGS IN THIS AGE GROUP.

Fig 12: Suicide rates among 15-24 year olds in England and Wales

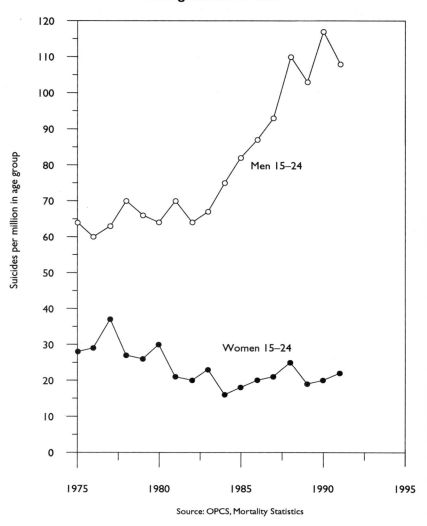

Source: OPCS, Mortality Statistics

Fig 12 shows the trends in suicide rates among young men and women. There was an alarming increase in suicides among young men from the mid 1980s. Although there was nothing so dramatic among young women, there is some evidence that a declining trend in their suicide rates was reversed over the same period.

4. Longer-Term Trends and Effects of Relative Deprivation

Some of the corrosive effects of increased relative deprivation take longer to show up than those we have looked at so far. Trends among the youngest children are most likely to be affected by short term circumstances. Amongst teenagers and older people there is an accumulation of experience: the psychological effects of socioeconomic processes have a longer history. For instance: while emotional damage in early childhood may result in behavioural problems at school, it is not till teens and early adulthood that similar problems will influence crime rates. The effects of family stress and emotional damage built up over the years to affect school performance, job prospects, and youth culture more widely. Because many of the longer term effects of changes in relative deprivation can appear as autonomous processes of cultural change, their causes are more easily obfuscated. Let us look at how long term trends in relative poverty might relate to trends in crime, drugs and depression.

The proportion of the population living in relative poverty has increased almost continuously since the early 1950s. Figure 13 shows Piachaud's data on changes in relative poverty between 1953 and 1983.[65] They have been updated to 1990/91 using figures from the Department of Social Security.[10] First, a few words about their interpretation. Clearly relative poverty could appear to increase just because definitions change. The strength of these figures is that Piachaud has attempted to apply the same relative standard all the way through. (He makes the same allowances for the numbers of people in each household as were made in the 1983 supplementary benefit scales and then uses the same proportions of personal disposable income for each household type at that date to define relative poverty at other dates.) What the graph shows then is the proportion of people in the lower tail of the income distribution at each date. It tells us nothing about changing income differentials among the rest of the population, and need be only partially consistent with the data shown in Figure 1. (What makes the trends shown there for the 1980s unique is that they show a growth in inequality among the population as a whole, rather than just the lengthening tail of poverty shown in Figure 13.) The last point is that the figures for 1953 and 1960 show the proportion of *households* in relative poverty are not comparable with those from 1973 onwards which cover *families*. A very rough adjustment for this difference would move the 1960 figure very much closer to the 1973 figure showing little growth in poverty between those dates.

Fig 13: Increasing percentage of household/families living in relative poverty

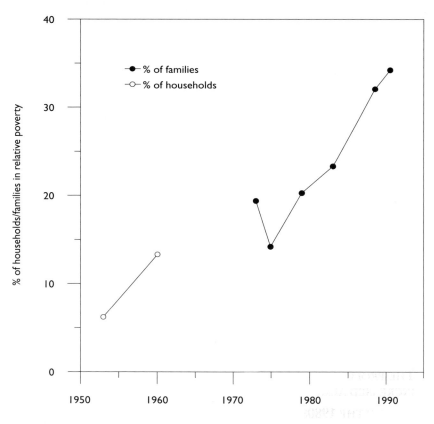

Source: Piachaud D, Poverty in Britain 1899–1983, *Journal of Social Policy*, 1988; 17: 335–49
(Updated from DSS, Households below average income 1979–1991)

Fig 13 records the growth of relative poverty in Britain since the early 1950s. The earliest two points, at the lower left, show the proportion of households in poverty. All the later figures show the proportion of families in poverty, so the two parts of the graph are not comparable. However, if earlier figures were available for families they would have shown much higher proportions in poverty initially and given the impression of a much smaller growth in poverty during the 1960s. The figures from 1970 onwards are comparable. Throughout the series relative poverty is defined as a constant proportion of average income after allowing for the number of people in each family or household. Although there has been almost a continuous rise in the proportion of the population in relative poverty during the second half of this century, the rate has been particularly rapid since the late 1970s.

The veracity of the longer-term trends in relative poverty is confirmed by the tendency for class differences in mortality to widen in step with them.[28] As well as the long-term widening, a smaller widening is apparent between 1961 and 1971, and it is possible to see a diminution in class differences in infant mortality differentials in the mid 1970s when relative poverty temporarily declined.[66]

There are several causes of the widening of income differences. In his analysis of increases in relative poverty up to 1983, Piachaud calculates that most of it is not the result of increases in the categories of the population in which poverty tends to be more common. Changes in the age structure and family composition of the population account for rather little of the increase. Changes in employment status are important at least towards the end of this analysis in 1983. Other studies which have covered the most recent period attribute the widening of income differentials to widening disparities in original earnings and to changes in taxes and benefits.[67][68] Half the widening is estimated to have come from tax and benefit changes – of which tax changes were the most important. Changes in the structure of economic activity – increases in unemployment, in self-employment and in the number of the elderly retired – were next most important. At the bottom of the income distribution these changes have had more effect than changes in the distribution of earnings. At the top, changes in earnings were more important.

THE PROPORTION OF PEOPLE LIVING IN RELATIVE POVERTY HAS INCREASED ALMOST CONTINUOUSLY SINCE THE 1950S.

DURING THE 1980S, INEQUALITY INCREASED ACROSS THE WHOLE POPULATION AT AN ACCELERATING RATE.

Crime

It is often suggested that crime is related to relative poverty and/or unemployment. Recently there has been some controversy as to what the trends in youth crime have been. After listening to expert opinion, the House of Commons Home Affairs Committee Report on *Juvenile Crime* came to no firm conclusions.[69] Although a large proportion of all crime is committed by young people, it is impossible to gain any clear knowledge of trends in juvenile crime as distinct from all crime.

Although the ages of those arrested and found guilty are known, the ages of people committing the unsolved majority of crime are unknown. Policy towards juvenile offenders has been changing rapidly. In 1983, of those boys 10 – 16 years old who either admitted guilt (a precondition for a caution) or were found guilty in court, 53 per cent were cautioned by the police. By 1990 this had risen to 75 per cent. Among girls the figures rose from 75 per cent in 1983 to 89 per cent in 1990.[70] It is likely that this increase in the use of cautions went with an increased tendency to take no formal action against younger children for less serious offences. Such changes almost certainly mean that trends in the total number of young people found guilty or cautioned are not an indication of the real trends in juvenile crime. The safest guide is probably to assume that juveniles contribute a constant proportion of all crime.

The trends in the total number of notifiable offences reported to the police since 1950 are shown in Figure 14. There has been a ten-fold increase in recorded crime and in recent years the annual additions to the total number of crimes recorded has been about equal to all known crime in the early 1950s. These changes are much too large to be attributed wholly to changes in police recording or the public's tendency to report crime.

A research report from the Home Office shows a close association between crime and the business cycle.[71] It showed a very robust statistical relationship between changes in consumer's expenditure per capita and crime. Property crime and violence had different relationships and lag periods, but the equations showed very clearly that annual fluctuations in crime were closely related to changes in personal income. Although it is a major step forward to show that crime is related to the socioeconomic environment, what this analysis did not do was provide any explanation for the long-term rise in crime.

Fig 14: Number of notifiable offences recorded by the police in England and Wales per 10,000 population

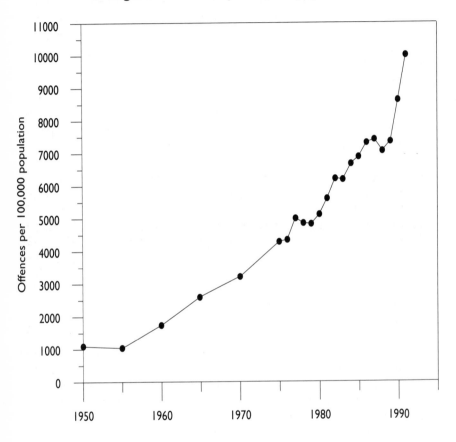

Source: Home Office, Criminal Statistics. HMSO; 1993

Fig 14 shows the almost continuous rise in crime since the mid 1950s. The increases in crime during the early 1990s were the biggest on record. The annual increases then exceeded the total crime rate in the early 1950s. Because a great deal of crime is unreported, some of the variations shown may reflect changes in reporting.

Almost the only developed country which appears not to have shared to some extent in the general rise in crime is Japan. Homicide, robbery, rape, violence and bodily injury have all shown a long-term decline.[72] Although many Japanese attribute the decline to their rapid economic growth, suggesting that robbery has decreased because rising incomes mean that there are fewer poor people who need to steal, this explanation sounds odd to Western ears. We have got used to thinking that somehow, as everyone has got better off, this has made us all more materialistic and selfish.

An alternative explanation for the differing trends lies less in what has been happening to economic growth and *absolute* living standards than in what has been happening to income distribution and trends in *relative* poverty. While Japan has experienced a long-term decline in income differences which, as we have seen, led to astonishingly rapid improvements in life expectancy, most other developed countries have seen either a worsening or little change in income distribution. An analysis of Japanese crime written by an author unaware of trends in Japanese income distribution, pointed out that the fastest declines in Japanese crime have taken place in the largest cities where crime rates were highest.[73] It cites evidence that with the passage of time Japanese crime has become less closely related to measures of deprivation. These are both patterns we would expect to find during a period of narrowing income differences if there were a component of crime related to relative deprivation. The component associated with deprivation would decrease, leaving other components of crime more predominant. The signs are clearly that this is what has happened. The only categories of crime which have shown any tendency to rise are the "white-collar" crimes classified in the Japanese statistics as "Intellectual offences".

The result is that Japanese women are able to walk home late at night in Tokyo without fear of attack and Japan has fewer muggings in a year than Britain has in a week.[74] Special videos have to be produced to warn unwary Japanese tourists travelling overseas not to leave their valuables unattended.

The House of Commons Home Affairs Committee report on *Juvenile Crime* says "there is obviously an unquestionable link in some cases between unemployment, hopelessness and crime" (p. xx). It goes on to say "A range of social and economic policies would undoubtedly make young people less likely to turn to crime" and warns "It is of no use to achieve economic success if moral bankruptcy comes in its wake"

(p. lxvi). In his last annual report the former Commissioner of the
Metropolitan Police, Sir Peter Imbert, said "The continuing growth of
crime is a fundamental concern which, in part, I attribute to the
marginalisation of some elements in our society. There is a need to offer
hope to those most disadvantaged if we are to see any reduction in
crime."[75] He said disadvantage and deprivation were factors "which we
ignore at our peril". The relationship between unemployment and crime
now seems to be sufficiently well established for senior civil servants to
advise ministers that "the single most effective form of intervention
would be the provision of employment to offenders".

CRIME IN THE UK FLUCTUATES WITH CHANGES IN PERSONAL
INCOME.

THE LONG-TERM RISE IN CRIME SINCE THE 1950S HAS
ACCOMPANIED A LONG-TERM INCREASE IN RELATIVE POVERTY.

JAPAN IS UNUSUAL AMONG DEVELOPED COUNTRIES IN HAVING
EXPERIENCED DECLINING CRIME RATES AND A LONG-TERM
DECLINE IN INCOME DIFFERENCES.

THE WEAKENING ASSOCIATION BETWEEN CRIME AND
DEPRIVATION IN JAPAN IS CONSISTENT WITH THE HYPOTHESIS
THAT A SIGNIFICANT COMPONENT OF CRIME IS RELATED TO
RELATIVE POVERTY.

Depression

An analysis of the lifetime experience of depression in different age
cohorts found strong evidence of an increase in depression among the
population. Results showed increased depression among younger adults,
particularly those born since World War II.[76] The evidence suggested
that an unknown period effect had been progressively increasing rates
of depression since W.W.II. The author claimed that similar trends had
been reported in suicide, in some forms of violent death and in drug
abuse. Although official statistics show increases between 1986 and
1989/90 in the rates of admission to mental hospitals for children
and adults up to the age of 34 years, it is not clear how the
figures are influenced by changes in the provision of other forms of
residential care.[77]

> **RATES OF DEPRESSION IN THE UK HAVE INCREASED PROGRESSIVELY SINCE WORLD WAR II.**

Drugs

Drug abuse is closely related to depression, unemployment and suicide. As well as showing a long-term rising trend, between 1983 and 1991 there was more than a doubling in drug dealing offences recorded by the police and the rate of drug offending among young people rose particularly steeply.[1 2] That these are not just changes in reporting can be seen from the four- to five-fold increase in deaths from sniffing glue and other volatile substances.[3] However, much of the increase in drug use was not among the most deprived. The use of several soft drugs became widespread in the youth culture of the later 1980s. The *National Audit* of the Institute for the Study of Drug Dependence says "the relatively stable youth drug use patterns of the mid 1980s were disturbed in the late '80s and by the '90s there was increased use of established drugs like cannabis, solvents, amphetamine, and magic mushrooms and an upsurge in the use of ecstasy and LSD".[78]

> **RATES OF DRUG ABUSE IN THE UK HAVE SHOWN A LONG-TERM INCREASE.**
>
> **THE INCREASE HAS BEEN PARTICULARLY STEEP SINCE 1983 AND IS NOT CONFINED TO THE MOST DEPRIVED PART OF THE POPULATION.**

Absolute poverty and relative deprivation

There was an almost continuous growth in average personal disposable income per capita during the 1980s (shown in Figure 15). According to Government figures, only the poorest 10 per cent of the population suffered a loss of real income between 1979 and 1990/91.[10] Their incomes went down by one per cent (14 per cent after allowing for housing costs). As these figures exclude homeless people they slightly underestimate the deterioration. The next poorest 10 per cent saw their incomes increase by six per cent (reduced to no increase after allowing for housing costs). The remaining 80 per cent of the population saw increases in their real incomes. Across the population as a whole the increases averaged out at 36 per cent between 1979 and 1990/91.

But even the poorest 10 per cent of the population who lost income saw improvements in their ownership of consumer durables over this period. The proportion with a fridge or freezer more than doubled, from 32 to 79 per cent.[10] The proportion with central heating rose from 42 to 72 per cent, and with telephones from 47 to 72 per cent. Thus even among the poorest there were improvements in access to household equipment.

These trends suggest that the average absolute standard of living does not hold the key to the sense of a profound deterioration in the social fabric of our society. This impression is confirmed by the international data on health, which is the easiest data to analyse as an indicator of the wider effects on welfare. The absence of a strong relationship between income and health between developed countries (as illustrated in Figure 10) is strong evidence that the *absolute* material standard of living no longer has a major influence on death rates in the rich developed countries.

That health is related to income *within* developed countries, but not to the large differences in average incomes which exist between them, could once have appeared as an inconsistency. In fact it provides additional confirmation that the health effects of income within countries is a function of the *relative* rather than the *absolute* standard of living. After societies have reached a certain level of affluence, the general increase in the absolute standard of living resulting from economic growth no longer makes much difference to health. However, the scale of relative deprivation (as measured by the income differences between people within the same society) continues to be a powerful determinant of health. Hence the close association between national mortality rates and measures of societal income distribution shown in Figures 6 – 9.

In the course of economic development the predominant position of material factors as determinants of health has given way to social factors. The point at which the vast majority of the population have access to the basic necessities is marked historically by the reversal in the social class distribution of the so-called "diseases of affluence". Once more common in the upper classes, at this key period in economic development the diseases of affluence (such as coronary heart disease and obesity) become the diseases of the poor in affluent societies.[82] This health transformation (the so-called "epidemiological transition") also sees the disappearance of the great infections – which were always associated with absolute poverty – as important causes of death. In Britain these changes were completed in the middle decades of the present century. Another marker is that since the 1950s there has been no further marked decline in the proportion of low birthweight babies: between six and seven per cent of babies have had birthweights below 2500g ever since.[83 84] Broadly similar changes have taken place in other developed societies at slightly different dates.

The central problem is then relative income. This report has not focused primarily on unemployment or homelessness because, in an important sense, unemployment is included in figures of income distribution or relative poverty, and homelessness is partly an expression of relative poverty. That is not to say that each of the components and effects of widening income differences does not have special implications, some of which are no doubt more devastating than others. However, for what the figures on trends in unemployment are worth, the unemployment rate rose during the early 1980s and fell during the later 1980s before rising again from 1990.[85]

Income distribution exercises its powerful influence on national mortality rates because it is an important determinant of the psychosocial welfare of the population. While there is no difficulty in understanding that widening income differences give rise to a variety of psychosocial and cultural processes which lead to a number of social ills, the psychosocial nature of the links with health are less obvious. However, there are a number of reasons for thinking that the same kinds of pathways are involved.

The fact that it is relative rather than absolute material standards which influence health means that cognitive and comparative would lead to a better estimate of life expectancy in a country than knowing the share of a smaller, more extreme group. This implies that life expectancy is affected by the relative incomes of a larger group than that included in conventional definitions of relative poverty.

A second indication that this relationship involves the health of a large proportion of the population is the fact that the international differences in average life expectancy associated with differences in income distribution are too large to be explained by changes in the health of a small minority alone. If the health disadvantage of social classes IV and V were totally removed, the resulting change in Britain's average life expectancy would not be large enough to raise its longevity to the level of the more egalitarian countries.

Thirdly, comparisons of the social class distribution of death rates in Britain and Sweden (as an example of a more egalitarian country) show not only that the mortality gradient in Sweden is much less steep, but also that death rates are lower in all classes. This is true for adult mortality rates as well as for the infant mortality rates which were shown in Figure 4.[79]

The fourth and final reason for thinking that income distribution affects the health of a large proportion of the population is that the mortality gradient in developed countries seems to go all the way up the social ladder. Health on each higher rung is better than on the rung below it. Thus, in a study of office-based civil servants in London, it was found that at every level in the occupational hierarchy more senior grades had lower death rates than more junior ones.[80 81] This is also shown in the US data illustrated in Figure 5.

The evidence that the health of a large proportion of the population is affected by this relationship rules out explanations exclusively in terms of small minorities such as unemployed or homeless people suffering the most extreme forms of deprivation. While such groups will contribute disproportionately to the relationship, they are too small a proportion of the population to account for it. If this is true for health, it may well be true for the other effects of relative deprivation.

THE ADVERSE HEALTH EFFECTS OF INCOME INEQUALITIES ARE SEEN AMONG A LARGE PROPORTION OF THE POPULATION, NOT MERELY THOSE NEAR THE BOTTOM OF THE INCOME SCALE.

Fig 15: Personal disposable income per capita, UK 1950-91

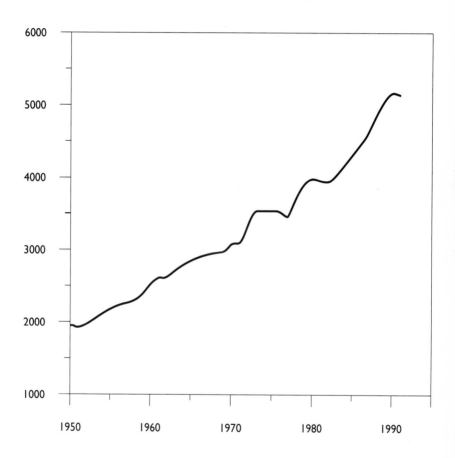

Fig 15 shows the growth in average incomes since 1950. It illustrates the increase in real purchasing power of average incomes after allowing for changes in prices, taxes and benefits.

5. Explanations

It is often said that it is necessary to show mechanism to establish causality and that association on its own is not enough. However this is not strictly true: randomised controlled trials come closer than any other scientific method to establishing causality while giving no clue as to mechanism. But in fact there is no shortage of possible mechanisms linking income distribution to a range of social consequences: the problem is choosing between them. Much of what follows consists therefore of looking at the evidence which indicates the kind of links which are most likely to be involved. It shows the kinds of processes which simultaneously link poorer health, less good school performance, and other aspects of the welfare of children and young people to income distribution.

What proportion of the population is affected?

It is often assumed that the damaging effects of widening income differences and increasing relative deprivation are confined to a minority in poverty. The data on mortality and life expectancy strongly suggest that this is not the case. Although Figures 7 and 9 show that there is a close relationship with the extent of relative poverty (as measured by the proportion of the population living on less than half the average income), total life expectancy at birth seems to be most closely related to the proportion of income received by the least well-off *half* of the population. If, for example, you take the proportion of income going to just the poorest 10 or 20 per cent of the population in each country, the relationship with life expectancy is less close. Taking the share of income going to the bottom 30, 40 and 50 per cent by adding successive deciles, shows that the relationship builds up to a maximum strength at the proportion of income going to the bottom 50 per cent of the population (about 60 per cent of households). [30] [35] In effect, knowing the income share of the bottom half of the population processes must be involved. Rather than people's material circumstances having a *direct physiological* impact on them – as with exposure to toxic materials for instance – what matters now is what people feel about their circumstances and what the differences in their circumstances makes them feel about themselves. This is a matter of how their circumstances compare with those of others. It is the social and psychological meanings attached to material differences which impact on health.

The primacy of "psychosocial" links, rather than direct physical links, with material differences is also implied by the fact that "inequalities" in health within the population are not merely differences between the health of a poor minority and the rest of the population. Health differences between groups near the top of the social ladder cannot be a matter of damp housing, poor diets or inadequate heating systems.

The same conclusion is suggested by the fact that although the population has grown richer and reduced the numbers in absolute deprivation during most decades since the middle of this century, health inequalities have, nevertheless, continued to widen.

The living standards of the least well-off 20 per cent of the population also point away from any suggestion that absolute deprivation continues to be the main determinant of the health disadvantage of a large proportion of the population. Table 1 shows that ownership of fridges and television sets is almost universal, and close to three-quarters of even the poorest 20 per cent of households have central heating, a freezer or fridge-freezer, a telephone and washing machine. This does not of course mean that no one in Britain goes without necessities – indeed a study of the working of the Social Fund found that a third of recipients said that they had to cut down on food, clothes and paying bills in order to repay loans to the Social Fund.[86] Nor should one forget the difficulty of maintaining these consumer durables on a small income. A washing machine pump replacement or a towed away car are financial disasters to many.

Table 1. Percentage in each income group with access to various consumer durables in 1992.

Income group	Bottom 20%	Bottom 50%	Total pop.
car or van	43	57	71
central heating	72	75	82
freezer or fridge-freezer	75	82	87
fridge or fridge-freezer	97	98	99
telephone	72	81	89
television	98	99	99
video	57	64	73
washing machine	84	89	92

However, given that the relationship between income distribution and health is likely to involve the health of a large proportion of the population, the fact that the ownership of consumer durables is as high as it is even among the poorest 20 per cent of families emphasises once again that we are not dealing with absolute deprivation.

Not only is a direct physiological or material link between ill-health and income unlikely among the better off, there is no indication that the primary role shifts from psychosocial to material influences even among the least well off. Although material influences on health get stronger among the least well off, so too does the sense of desperation, anxiety and depression. Among homeless families in bed-and-breakfast accommodation, 44 per cent of women said that they were unhappy most of the time, 41 per cent were tired most of the time, 35 per cent often lost their temper, 34 per cent could not sleep at night, 33 per cent said their children got on top of them, and 24 per cent said they burst into tears for no reason.[87] Given that general happiness – or life satisfaction – is a good predictor of longevity and that a wide range of adverse psychosocial factors has been shown to make a substantial difference to health, it is to be expected that the psychosocial effects on health will be strongest where relative deprivation is greatest.

THERE IS STRONG EVIDENCE THAT INCREASES IN THE *ABSOLUTE* MATERIAL STANDARD OF LIVING NO LONGER HAVE A MAJOR INFLUENCE ON AVERAGE DEATH RATES IN THE RICH DEVELOPED COUNTRIES.

HOWEVER, THE INCOME *DIFFERENCES* BETWEEN PEOPLE WITHIN THE SAME SOCIETY CONTINUE TO BE A POWERFUL DETERMINANT OF HEALTH.

INCOME DISTRIBUTION AFFECTS BOTH HEALTH AND SOCIAL TRENDS THROUGH THE EFFECTS IT HAS ON THE PSYCHOSOCIAL WELFARE OF THE POPULATION.

EVEN AMONG THE POOREST IN SOCIETY, THE PSYCHOSOCIAL EFFECTS OF INCOME INEQUALITY ARE A STRONG DETERMINANT OF HEALTH.

Psychosocial influences on health

Having established that the evidence strongly suggests that the health effects of income distribution involve *comparative* social and cognitive processes, rather than the direct effects of material standards, we can now go on to see what studies have to say about the biological plausibility of such a link.

The physiological pathways by which psychosocial factors may exert a major influence on mortality have been described in the scientific literature. They involve both the immune and endocrine systems, and are capable of affecting infections, cardiovascular diseases and cancers.[88 89 90 91]

The effects are powerful enough to be measured quite easily and there are examples of experimental as well as observational studies which show the processes at work. For example, in one experiment volunteers were given nasal drops containing various strains of cold viruses while controls were given pure distilled water. The proportion developing "clinical colds" was directly related to psychological measures of their stress levels and varied from 27 per cent among the lowest stress group to 47 per cent among the highest.[92] Observational studies have also demonstrated the effect of stress on the immune system.[93]

So-called "natural" experiments have repeatedly shown the power of psychosocial factors on physical health. One example showed the effect on the health of residents when their housing estate was threatened with demolition.[95] In another, people in Bristol whose houses where flooded in 1969 were found to have a 50 per cent higher mortality rate during the following year compared with controls.[96] A study of the health effects of job losses resulting from a factory closure found that health began to deteriorate as soon as redundancies were first announced – before people actually became unemployed.[97] This again testifies to the power of psychosocial influences on health. Similarly, an Australian study of unemployment found health more closely related to the subjective experience of financial strain than to actual income.[98]

Progress has also been made in identifying the particular social and psychological characteristics which seem to have an effect on health. Workplace studies conducted in Sweden, the United States, Germany and Britain of health among different grades of employees have emphasised the importance of three aspects of the psychosocial work environment.[80 99 100 101] These are the amount of control people have over their work, the pressure of work and the social support they get from colleagues.

These three factors are likely to apply to people's domestic circumstances as much as to their working conditions. Indeed, numerous studies have confirmed the important beneficial effects on health of more and better quality social contacts between people – regardless of work.[102] Good friendships are often seen as protective against the effects of stress. One study provided evidence that they are also specifically protective against the effects of stress induced by economic hardship.[103] Several studies have shown that poorer people and people in lower status occupations are likely to have less social contact.[104 105]

Like social support, most of the psychosocial circumstances deleterious to health are more likely to occur in relatively deprived circumstances. Others studies designed to show the links between relative deprivation and health have shown – not unexpectedly – that deprivation causes stress,[103] that socioeconomic status affects "fatalism" and attributional style,[106] that economic hardship reduces people's ability to fulfil their roles – whether as "breadwinner" or "homemaker" – and so causes depression.[107]

Before leaving the question of the nature of the links between relative deprivation and health, it is worth pointing out that the most well known risk factors play only a minor role. Several studies have, for instance, concluded that perhaps only 20 per cent of the social class differences in heart disease death rates are explained by the combined effects of all the most important known risk factors (such as high blood pressure, smoking, obesity and high blood cholesterol levels) for heart disease[107][108]. Of course part, even of that 20 per cent, may be attributable to psychosocial influences insofar as smoking, blood pressure and dietary choices may be influenced by morale and sense of control.[109][110]

MEDICAL RESEARCH AND "NATURAL" EXPERIMENTS CONFIRM THAT PHYSICAL HEALTH IS STRONGLY INFLUENCED BY PSYCHO-LOGICAL FACTORS SUCH AS STRESS, LACK OF SUPPORT, FINANCIAL INSECURITY, LOW SELF-ESTEEM AND LOW SENSE OF CONTROL.

SUCH FACTORS OCCUR MOST FREQUENTLY IN RELATIVELY DEPRIVED CIRCUMSTANCES.

Social processes

The psychosocial impact of income distribution on national death rates testifies to the extent of the social dislocation caused by widening income differences. It tells us that human beings are more sensitive to inequality than had previously been recognised.

But the relationship between increasing income differentials and the various social problems it creates is not necessarily a simple one. A large number of different pathways are involved in the links with crime, child abuse, reading standards, school expulsions, drug taking, child prostitution and health problems of different kinds in different age groups. Because the relationships are not always clear and simple they are denied as an excuse for inaction, and the social and financial costs continue to increase. However, there can be no doubt that relative deprivation is a component in all these outcomes and has contributed to the statistical trends we have seen in recent years.

Each of the various forms relative deprivation can take have a wide variety of effects. For instance, when people fear unemployment or losing their homes because they cannot keep up with mortgage payments, the stress may result in increased domestic conflict, divorce, heart attack, depression, emotional disturbances in the children, increased use of alcohol, child neglect as parents work longer hours, social security fraud, theft and so on.

That they have some common roots is also shown by the extent to which the various different problems we have discussed overlap, and how one is a risk factor for another. The links between them are familiar. Unemployment and low income lead to increases in family conflict which increases the chances of emotional disturbance and behavioural disorders among children. A study of the effects of unemployment on marriage found that half the couples reported an increase in the number of arguments and a third said that one or other partner had left home temporarily or contemplated doing so.[111] Social life was curtailed and their circle of friends shrank. The effect of unemployment on marriage was particularly severe among young couples with children. This, and other more direct effects of deprivation on the home environment, increase the likelihood of educational impairment among children. The parents of children on Child Protection Registers are much less likely than others to be employed. The sources of stress contributing to child abuse which are most frequently recorded by the workers who register each case were the same year after year: marital problems, debts and unemployment.[4]

The contribution which domestic conflict makes to emotional disturbance and later delinquency among children is also well known. A quarter of all children running away from home were found to have previous criminal convictions and many had been regular truants from school.[112] Later on we find a link between crime and mental and emotional problems. A third of 16 – 18 year old men given criminal sentences are classified as having "primary psychiatric disorders".[54] The links between low income, depression and violence in adults and later delinquency in their children has recently been drawn together to show how the recent rapid increases in violent crime can be explained.[114]

The effects of income distribution on stress in families and the emotional development of children is not confined to the relatively poor any more than it is only the poor who get into debt or financial difficulties. As well as adding to stress and domestic conflict at home, it also increases the pressure on parents – particularly lone parents – to find work, even when the hours squeeze the time left for child care. Low pay means that people with jobs tend to work longer hours where they can. The upward shift in the hours people worked can be seen during the 1980s until the trend was halted by the recession of the early

1990s.[114] There is growing international concern about the effects of child neglect resulting from increased relative deprivation and changes in the job market.[21] The proportion of women going back to work within nine months of giving birth increased during the 1980s from 25 to 45 per cent.[114]

Inadequate resources, financial stress, an unemployed husband at home, or an inability to afford housing with adequate space for a family, all increase the frequency of domestic conflict and family rows. Domestic conflict is an important cause of emotional disturbance in children which in turn has immediate as well as longer-term effects. Although family rows occur throughout society, there is no doubt that they are harder to avoid as stress from other sources increases. It is, after all, easier to avoid getting angry with a child who loses a coat or breaks something if you can easily afford to replace it and have not already faced several rebuffs during the day.

Another important pathway is linked to low self-esteem, and to a sense of failure and inadequacy, to which a relatively low income predisposes people. In the eyes of society how well-off you are appears as an expression of your ability and value as a member of society: implying that poorer people are of less account. This is closely related to the notion of respectability which, for many, is synonymous with social status and looking "respectable". Self-esteem for others may be equally dependent on having the right make of trainers or tee-shirts. With the lack of self-confidence which is exacerbated by relative deprivation, comes an atrophying of friendships and the social contacts which have been found to be protective against the effects of stress. It is difficult not to suggest that a sense of depression and inadequacy, inactivity and eating for comfort, contributed to the dramatic increases in obesity among men aged 16 – 64 and among women 35 – 64 years. Between 1987 and 1991 obesity almost doubled among men and increased by about a third among the women.[115]

As the international health evidence makes clear, it is not just a poor minority of the population whose health is affected by income differentials, and it is not just a matter of need. Though that is where the damage may start, the ripples spread much more widely, eroding social values, attitudes and social relations throughout society.

The effects of increases in relative poverty and deprivation affect the sense of security among the majority of the population. The more unemployment, homelessness, houses repossessed, and poverty there is, the greater will be the sense of anxiety and insecurity among the population at large. The sense of security which comes from knowing that there are adequate pensions, that high quality medical care is available to all, that there are job vacancies within reach, and that an adequate safety net exists to prevent destitution, is replaced by a growing sense of insecurity as these guarantees crumble. If things go wrong there is further to fall and the risks of daily life are more worrying.

At the same time, a less caring society redefines human relations. Social norms are redrawn. We become familiar with the coexistence of begging and homelessness alongside wealth and our humanity is subtly redefined. Greater insecurity obliges everyone to look to their own needs in disregard for those of others. Increasing crime means that we see others as a threat to our own welfare. People become fearful on the streets and our assumptions about how we relate to each other change. Where once the welfare apparatus of the state had stood as a clear statement of our mutual responsibilities to our fellow human beings, their decline now stands as a denial of that responsibility.

There are also problems of the perceived legitimacy and fairness of social institutions and of the social structure as income distribution widens. A law abiding society depends to a large extent on the social organisation being seen as a system which operates fairly and enables people to live satisfactory lives in accordance with its rules. Where people feel their paths are blocked, that they are denied opportunities and treated unfairly, breaking the law ceases to be a moral issue and depends instead on a calculation of risks and benefits. The gradual transformation of a society, which had at least some of the attributes of a community which cared for its members, into a collection of individuals related only through the pursuit of material self-interest, leads to further decay of the social fabric.

To dismiss issues of relative deprivation and relative poverty as the "politics of greed" or of "envy" is as inaccurate as it is insulting. The processes have more in common with the situation in parts of the world where remnants of tribal societies have become marginalised and impoverished by more powerful modern societies. As their culture and way of life is undermined and becomes unworkable, people are left without the coherent cultural system capable of providing meaningful roles and the social basis of self-respect. Those who can leave do; many of the rest sink into listlessness, despair, alcoholism and self-destruction. The effects of relative poverty in metropolitan societies are not so different.

FINANCIAL HARDSHIP INCREASES THE RISKS OF FAMILY CONFLICT AND ALSO OF EMOTIONAL DISTURBANCE AND DELINQUENCY IN CHILDREN.

DEBT, UNEMPLOYMENT, HOMELESSNESS, LOW SELF-ESTEEM AND THE LOSS OF SOCIAL CONTACT IMPOSE STRESSES WHICH CONTRIBUTE TO THE DAMAGE CATALOGUED IN THIS REPORT.

GREATER MATERIAL INSECURITY, A SENSE OF INJUSTICE AND A GROWTH OF ANTI-SOCIAL TENDENCIES TAKE THEIR TOLL THROUGHOUT SOCIETY.

6. Conclusions

This report has drawn attention to the unexpectedly serious social repercussions of widening income differences and increasing material insecurity. Financial stress and insecurity, arising from threats to jobs and the increasing difficulty of maintaining relative living standards as income differences widen, are a major addition to the pressures of family life. They affect children's emotional development and rebound on social attitudes and behaviour more widely as well as calling into question the legitimacy of social institutions.

We have traced some of the statistical links between increasing relative deprivation and growing psychosocial problems among young people. It is not intended to suggest that all these problems are wholly due to widening income differentials and relative poverty. What the evidence shows is that, directly or indirectly, relative deprivation is an important contributor to the rising trends in all of them.

Four points about the relationship between income distribution and aspects of psychosocial welfare should be borne in mind. First, there can be long-term and short-term effects of increased relative deprivation: not all effects will show the short-term associations we have seen in mortality data and in reading scores. Secondly, although the effects of relative deprivation will be more common further down the social scale, they will not be confined to the very poorest in society. Thirdly, there are other important influences on the trends which will add to, modify or counteract the effects of relative deprivation. Lastly, relative deprivation itself comes in a variety of economic and material forms, from homelessness to a lack of educational opportunities, each of which impinges on people in different ways.

The costs of failure to solve these problems are enormous. In the United States, where relative poverty has also worsened dramatically in recent years, the death rate in both sexes and at most ages – except the youngest – is higher in Harlem, New York, than it is in rural

Bangladesh.[116] The greatest single cause of the excess mortality is heart disease. Although the death rates from drugs and violence have not yet overtaken it, both are reflections of the antisocial forces which can arise where people feel the system has ceased to work for them. So disabling are these trends that the control of drugs and violence within black communities is increasingly seen by black leaders as a precondition for political and economic emancipation.

As Donnison has pointed out, the kinds of social problems to which a maldistribution of income give rise are likely to be shaped by a number of factors including the demographic characteristics of each neighbourhood.[117] An area with a large number of lone parents will, as a consequence of their poverty, have a lot of debt problems, higher social security fraud and depression, and the schools will have to cope with more children with behavioural and learning difficulties. A poor area with a high proportion of old people will have high levels of loneliness, dementia, chronic disease and disability, high demands for health and community services and a lack of the social infrastructure able to provide care and support to elderly people living alone. Areas in which there is a high proportion of young men without jobs will be characterised by high crime rates, violence and drug use.

Each kind of area and each kind of problem gives rise to its own set of needs, but without very substantial increases in resources – both for the poor themselves and for the agencies trying to provide services – significant progress is unlikely. The results of working on any single consequence of widening differentials will be limited by the way each is embedded in a network of other constraints. Each problem is exacerbated by the existence of others. The problems of poor lone parents and unemployed young people are made worse by the wider setting of disadvantage: by the lack of good public transport, by the boredom of life on large estates, by high rates of unemployment, by the presence of drug pushers, by the lack of good educational opportunities and by so many other aspects of an impoverished material and social infrastructure. On many estates there are growing signs of antagonism, not towards the rich living safely the other side of town, but to the teachers, doctors, bus drivers and others whose job it is to provide services.

The responses to such circumstances are, as Donnison again points out, not determined in a totally predictable, deterministic way, but are chosen and shaped by individuals, families and communities.

Occasionally the social resources of confidence, energy and hope will be sufficient to lead a community out of antisocial behaviour, despair and apathy, and into a more positive cycle of creative activity, self-organisation and political involvement which could build the missing social infrastructure and begin to repair the damage: but much depends on people's success in bringing new resources into their community.

Operating at distinct levels, central and local government, health authorities, employers in public and private institutions, people working in communities and neighbourhoods, all have a role in repairing the damage. We need national policies to reduce income differentials through taxes and benefits, through economic and employment policies and through education and training. Organisations which employ people can create new jobs, increase job security and provide improved access for low paid employees to education and training on and off the job; they can experiment with more egalitarian working environments and they can reduce pay differentials. At the level of local government, housing provision, public services and the quality of the environment should all be addressed as matter of priority.

It must not be forgotten that these problems are rooted in the antisocial extent of material inequalities. Governments must bear the primary responsibility for the development of policies which can reverse the process of social waste. They need to act to bring together the social and economic costs for four reasons: to prevent the wastage of human life and human potential; because high quality human capital is now essential for economic growth; because the quality of a society's social fabric is now crucial to the quality of life of the population as a whole; and because the burden of social failure imposes an intolerable burden on public services and on the Exchequer – reflected in rising costs of health services, of crime control, of social security dependence, of vandalism, remedial education and so on.

In the short-term, income has to be redistributed through taxes and benefits. Later a better educated population and better economic performance will diminish differentials in pre-tax incomes. Where human resources are all-important, a social strategy now provides the essential underpinning of an economic strategy. Among OECD countries, those with narrower income differences tend to have faster rates of productivity growth.[118] Similarly, among a wider group of nations, there is a statistical association between narrower income differences and higher rates of investment.[119] All eight of the most rapidly growing south-east Asian economies reduced their income differentials between 1960 and 1980 and now have narrower income differences than elsewhere.[120] [121] These findings not only fit the belief that modern economic growth depends on a highly educated and adaptable labour force, but they also put paid to the idea that redistribution and growth are incompatible.

Until recently, few would have predicted the extent of the devastating social effects of a widening income distribution. As well as trying to repair the damage and making sure it never happens again, there is a deeper message to be learnt. That inequality should have such powerful psychosocial effects shows the crucial importance of the wider social dimension of human life. We are not merely economic beings, with material needs, motivated by material gain. Nor are our social needs limited to those met by domestic life and relationships. Vitally important is the way we fit into a wider structure of meaning, fulfilling roles from which we derive a sense of self-worth and experience ourselves as valued members of society. The neglect of this social dimension of life has reached a point where it blights the quality of life for all of us.

References

1. Home Office. *Criminal Statistics for England and Wales 1991*. HMSO 1993.

2. *The NCH Fact File: children in Britain 1992*. p. 64. National Children's Homes, London 1992. Homelessness figures p. 34; drug abuse figures p. 64.

3. Taylor JC, Norman CL, Griffiths JM, Anderson HR, Ramsey JD. *Trends in deaths associated with abuse of volatile substances 1971 – 1991*. Dept. of Public Health Sciences and the Toxicology Unit, St. George's Hospital Medical School, London 1993.

4. Creighton SJ. *Child abuse trends in England and Wales 1988 – 90*. NSPCC 1992.

5. Department of Health. *Children in care of local authorities. Year ending 31st March 1991*. England. HMSO 1993.

6. Gorman T. Fernandes C. *Reading in recession*. National Federation of Educational Research, Slough 1992.

7. Advisory Centre for Education, *Findings from ACE investigations into exclusions*. ACE, London 1993.

8. OPCS, Mortality Statistics. HMSO.

9. Rutter M. Services for children with emotional disorders. *Young Minds Newsletter*, 1991; 9: 1 – 5. National Association for Child and Family Mental Health.

10. Department of Social Security, *Households below average income 1979 – 1990/1*. HMSO 1993.

11. *Family Policy Bulletin*, December 1991. Family Policy Studies Centre.

12. Joseph Rowntree Foundation, *Social Policy Research Findings,* No. 37, May 1993.

13. OPCS, *Birth Statistics.* Series FM1 No.20. HMSO 1993.

14. Burghes L. *One-parent families: policy options for the 1990s.* Family Policy Studies Centre and Joseph Rowntree Foundation 1993.

15. Ferri E. *Growing up in a one-parent family.* NFER Publishing 1976.

16. McLanahan S. Family structure and the reproduction of poverty. *American Journal of Sociology* 1985; 90: 873 – 901.

17. Ferri E, Robinson H. *Coping alone.* NFER, 1976.

18. Wadsworth M, Maclean M, Kuh D, Rodgers B. Children of divorced and separated parents: summary and review of findings from a long-term follow-up study in the UK. *Family Practice* 1990; 7: 104 – 9.

19. Burghes L. *Lone parenthood and family disruption: the outcomes for children.* Family Policy Studies Centre, London 1994.

20. Kiernan K, Estaugh V. *Cohabitation, extra-marital childbearing and social policy.* Family Policy Studies Centre, London 1993.

21. Hewlett SA. *Child neglect in rich nations.* UNICEF, New York 1993.

22. Wilkinson RG. Social class differences in infant mortality. Letter. *British Medical Journal* 1992; 305: 1227.

23. Whitehead M. *The health divide.* Penguin Books, Harmondsworth 1992.

24. Mackenbach JP, Bouvier-Colle MH, Jougla E. "Avoidable" mortality and health services: a review of aggregate data studies. *Journal of Epidemiology and Community Health* 1990; 44: 106 – 11.

25. Davey Smith G, Shipley MJ, Rose G. Magnitude and causes of socioeconomic differentials in mortality: further evidence from the Whitehall Study. *Journal of Epidemiology and Community Health* 1990; 44: 265 – 70.

26. Power C, Manor O, Fox AJ, Fogelman K. Health in childhood and social inequalities in health in young adults. *Journal of the Royal Statistical Society* 1990; 153: 17 – 28.

27. Fox J, Goldblatt P, Jones D. Social class mortality differentials: artefact, selection or life circumstances? In: *Longitudinal study 1971 – 1981*. OPCS series LS no.6. London, HMSO 1990: 99 – 108.

28. Wilkinson RG. Class mortality differentials, income distribution and trends in poverty 1921 – 1981. *Journal of Social Policy* 1989; 18(3): 307 – 35.

29. Kunst AE, Mackenbach JP. The size of mortality differences associated with educational level. A comparison of nine industrialized countries. In press: *American Journal of Public Health* (forthcoming 1994)

30. Wilkinson RG. Income distribution and life expectancy. *British Medical Journal* 1992; 304: 165 – 68.

31. Wennemo I. Infant mortality, public policy and inequality — a comparison of 18 industrialised countries 1950 – 85. *Sociology of Health and Illness* 1993; 15: 429 – 46.

32. Wilkinson RG. Income and health. In: *Health, wealth and poverty*. Medical World / SHA, London 1993.

33. Marmot MG, Davey Smith G. Why are the Japanese living longer? *British Medical Journal* 1989; 299: 1547 – 51.

34. Marmot MG, McDowall ME. Mortality decline and widening social inequalities. *Lancet* 1986; ii: 274 – 76.

35. Wilkinson RG. The impact of income inequality on life expectancy. In: Platt S, Thomas H, Scott S, Williams G (eds) *Locating health: sociological and historical explorations*. Avebury, Aldershot 1993.

36. Department of Health. *On the state of the public health. Annual report of the Chief Medical Officer 1990.* HMSO, London 1991.

37. Dunnell K. Deaths among 15 – 44 year olds. *Population Trends* 1991; 64: 38 – 43.

38. Woodroffe C, Glickman M, Barker B, Power C (eds) *Children, teenagers and health.* Open University Press, Buckinghamshire 1993.

39. Greater Glasgow Health Board. *The annual report of the Director of Public Health 1991/2.* Greater Glasgow Health Board 1993.

40. Phillimore P, Beattie A, Townsend P. The widening gap. Inequality of health in northern England, 1981 – 1991. *British Medical Journal,* 1994; 308: 1125-8.

41. Gorman T, Fernandes C. *Reading in recession.* National Federation of Educational Research, Slough 1992. (Gorman and Fernandes include a report of the anonymous research mentioned above.)

42. Croydon Education Authority. *Reading competence at age 7.* London Borough of Croydon, undated.

43. Lake M. Surveying all the factors. *Language and Learning* 1991; June No. 6.

44. Office for Standards in Education. *Access and achievement in urban education.* HMSO 1993.

45. Morris J, Blane D. Wasting children? *Journal of Epidemiology and Community Health* 1994, Forthcoming.

46. Power C, Manor O, Fox J. *Health and Class.* Chapman and Hall, London 1991.

47. Case R. Personal communication. Results of the Third International Math and Science Test. Institute of Child Study, Faculty of Education, University of Toronto.

48. Fraser C. The follow-up study: psychological aspects. In: Illsley R, Mitchell RG (eds) *Low birth weight: a medical, psychological and social study.* Wiley, Chichester 1984.

49. The Audit Commission and Her Majesty's Inspectorate, *Getting in on the Act. Provision for pupils with special educational needs: the national picture.* HMSO 1992.

50. The Advisory Centre for Education, *Findings from the ACE investigation into exclusions.* ACE, London 1993.

51. Office for Standards in Education, *Education for disaffected pupils.* HMSO 1992.

52. Bennathan M, Smith H. The state of services for children in London. *Young Minds Newsletter* 1991; 8: 10 – 12.

53. Bentham M. The care and education of troubled children. *Young Minds Newsletter* 1992; 10: 1 – 7.

54. Kurtz Z. Needs assessment and commissioning for mental health care for children and young people. *Young Minds Newsletter*, 1992; 12: 14 – 15.

55. Department of the Environment, *Homelessness Statistics.* HMSO 1991

56. *Building Societies Yearbook 1993/94.* As quoted in: *Moneywise,* October 1993, p. 36.

57. Maclagan I. *Four years' severe hardship.* Youthaid, Coalition on Young People and Social Security, Barnardo's, London 1993.

58. Coalition on Young People and Social Security. Young people and severe hardship. *Childright,* 1992; 83: 16 – 18.

59. Greve J. *Homelessness in Britain.* Joseph Rowntree Memorial Trust 1991.

60. Andrews K, Jacobs J. *Punishing the poor: poverty under Thatcher.* Macmillan, London 1990.

61. Killeen D. *Estranged: homeless 16 and 17 year olds and the Social Security Act 1988.* Shelter, 1988.

62. Platt S, Kreitman N. Trends in parasuicide and unemployment among men in Edinburgh, 1968—82. *British Medical Journal* 1984; 289: 1029 – 32.

63. Low Pay Unit. Taking the bloom off youth. *The New Review*, 1992; 15: 13 – 16.

64. Brown G, Harris T. *Social origins of depression*, Tavistock, London 1978.

65. Piachaud D. Poverty in Britain 1899 to 1983. *Journal of Social Policy* 1988; 17: 335 – 49.

66. Wilkinson RG. Income and mortality In: Wilkinson RG (ed) *Class and health: research and longitudinal data.* Tavistock 1986.

67. Johnson P, Webb S. Explaining the growth in UK income inequality: 1979 – 88. *Economic Journal* 1993; 103: 429 – 35.

68. Fritzell J. Income inequality trends in the 1980s: a five country comparison. *Acta Sociologica* 1993; 36: 47 – 62.

69. House of Commons Home Affairs Committee. *Juvenile Offenders*, Vol.1. HMSO 1993.

70. NACRO. Some facts about juvenile crime. *Nacro Briefing*, November 1992.

71. Field S. *Trends in crime and their interpretation.* Home Office Research and Planning Unit Report. HMSO, London 1990.

72. *Japan Statistical Yearbook 1990.* Statistics Bureau, Management and Coordination Agency.

73. Clifford W. *Crime control in Japan.* Lexington Books, London 1976.

74. *A necessary evil.* Radio broadcast presented by Phillip Short, produced by Donald McCleod. BBC Radio 4, 1992.

75. Kirby T. Imbert links rise in crime rate with social deprivation: final report of the retiring Metropolitan Police Commissioner. *The Independent* 30 July 1992.

76. Klerman GL. The current age of youthful melancholia: evidence for increase in depression among adolescents and young adults. *British Journal of Psychiatry.* 1988; 152: 4 – 14.

77. Department of Health. *Health and personal social services statistics for England 1992.* HMSO 1992.

78. Institute for the Study of Drug Dependence. *National audit of drug misuse in Britain 1992.* ISDD, 1992

79. Vegero D, Lundberg O. Health inequalities in Britain and Sweden. *Lancet* 1989; 2: 35 – 36.

80. Marmot MG, Davey Smith G, Stansfield S et al. Health inequalities among British civil servants: the Whitehall II study. *Lancet* 1991; 337: 1387 – 93.

81. Marmot MG, Rose G, Shipley M, Hamilton PJS. Employment grade and coronary heart disease in British civil servants. *Journal of Epidemiology and Community Health* 1978; 32: 244 – 49.

82. Marmot MG, Adelstein A, Robinson N, Rose G. Changing social class distribution of heart disease. *British Medical Journal* 1978; ii: 1109 – 12.

83. Macfarlane A, Mugford M. *Birth counts: statistics of pregnancy and childbirth.* HMSO 1984.

84. Power C. National trends in birthweight and future adult disease. *British Medical Journal,* Forthcoming: accepted Nov 1993.

85. Central Statistical Office *Economic Trends, Annual Supplement 1993.* HMSO, 1993.

86. Huby M, Dix G. *Evaluating the Social Fund.* HMSO, London 1992.

87. Conway J et al. *Prescriptions for poor health: the crisis for homeless families.* London Food Commission, Maternity Alliance, SHAC, Shelter 1988.

88. Henry JP. The relation of social to biological processes in disease. *Social Science and Medicine* 1982.

89. Kaplan HB, Social psychology of the immune system: a conceptual framework and review of the literature. *Social Science and Medicine* 1991; 33: 909 – 23.

90. Sterling P, Eyer J. Biological basis of stress-related mortality. *Social Science and Medicine*. 1981; 15E: 3 – 42.

91. Cox T, Mackay C. Psychosocial factors and psychophysiological mechanisms in the aetiology and development of cancers. *Social Science and Medicine* 1982; 16: 381 – 96.

92. Cohen S, Tyrrell DAJ, Smith AP. Psychological stress and susceptibility to the common cold. *New England Journal of Medicine* 1991; 325: 606 – 12.

93. Heisel JS, Locke SE, Kraus LJ, Williams RM. Natural killer cell activity and MMPI scores of a cohort of college students. *American Journal of Psychiatry* 1986; 143: 1382 – 86.

94. Halpern DS, Reid J. Effect of unexpected demolition announcement on health of residents. *British Medical Journal* 1992; 304: 1229 – 30.

95. Conduit EH. If A-B does not predict heart disease, why bother with it? A clinician's view. *British Journal of Medical Psychology* 1992; 65: 289 – 96.

96. Beale N, Nethercott S. Job-loss and family morbidity: a study of factory closure. *Journal of the Royal College of General Practitioners* 1988; 35: 510 – 14.

97. Ullah P. The association between income, financial strain and psychological well-being among unemployed youths. *Journal of Occupational Psychology* 1990; 63: 317 – 30.

98. Johnson JV, Hall EM. Job strain, work place social support, and cardiovascular disease: a cross-sectional study of a random sample of the Swedish working population. *American Journal of Public Health* 1988; 78: 1336 – 42.

99. Karasek RA et al. Job characteristics in relation to the prevalence of myocardial infarction in the U.S. *American Journal of Public Health* 1988; 78: 910 – 18.

100. Siegrist J, Peter R, Junge A, Cremer P, Seidel D. Low status control, high effort at work and ischaemic heart disease: prospective evidence from blue-collar men. *Social Science and Medicine* 1990; 31: 1127 – 34.

101. House JS, Landis KR, Umberson D. Social relationships and health. *Science*. 1988; 241: 540 – 5.

102. Whelan CT. The role of social support in mediating the psychological consequences of economic stress. *Sociology of Health and Illness* 1993; 15: 86 – 101.

103. Townsend P. *Poverty in the United Kingdom*. Penguin, Harmondsworth. 1979.

103. Marmot MG. Social inequalities in mortality: the social environment. In: Wilkinson RG (ed) *Class and health: research and longitudinal data*. Tavistock, London 1986.

105. Wheaton B. The sociogenesis of psychological disorder: an attributional theory. *Journal of Health and Social Behaviour* 1980; 21: 100 – 23.

106. Ross CE, Huber J. Hardship and depression. *Journal of Health and Social Behaviour* 1985; 26: 312 – 27.

107. Marmot MG, Shipley MJ, Rose G. Inequalities in death – specific explanations of a general pattern? *Lancet* 1984; i: 1003 – 6.

108. Pocock SJ, Shaper AG, Cook DG, Phillips AN, Walker M. Social class differences in ischaemic heart disease in British men. *Lancet* 1987; ii: 197 – 201.

109. Action on Smoking and Health. *Her share of misfortune*. ASH, London 1993.

110. Wilson SH, Walker GM. *Unemployment and health: a review*. Public Health 1993; 107: 153 – 62.

111. Burgoyne J. Unemployment and married life. *Unemployment Bulletin* 1985; 18: 7 – 10.

112. Abrahams C, Mungall R, National Children's Homes, The Police Foundation. *Runaways: exploding the myths.* NCH, London 1992.

113. James O. *Violence against the person since 1987: socioeconomic and familial origins of its unprecedented rise in England and Wales.* (Forthcoming).

114. Hewitt P. *About time: the revolution in work and family life.* Rivers Oram Press, London 1993.

115. OPCS. *Health Survey for England 1991.* HMSO 1993.

116. McCord C, Freeman HP. Excess mortality in Harlem. *New England Journal of Medicine* 1990; 322: 173 – 77.

117. Donnison D. Citizenship and civic leadership. Unpublished paper presented at a Fabian Society seminar on social justice, December 1993.

118. Milliband D, Glyn A. (eds) *Paying for inequality: the economic cost of social injustice.* Rivers Oram Press, London 1994.

119. Alesina A, Perotti R. *Income distribution, political instability, and investment.* NBER Working Paper 4486. Cambridge, Mass. 1993.

120. World Bank. *The East Asian Miracle.* Oxford University Press, 1993.

121. Birdsall N, Ross D, Sabot R. *Inequality and growth reconsidered.* Paper presented at the Annual Conference of the American Economic Association, Boston 1994.